RHINO 2017

RHINO: The Poetry Forum, Inc. is
supported in part by grants from the
Illinois Arts Council, a state agency,
Poets & Writers, Inc., and
The MacArthur Funds for Arts & Culture
at The Richard H. Driehaus Foundation.

RHINO is published annually and
considers submissions of poetry, flash fiction/
short-shorts, and translations.
Regular reading period: April 1 – July 31.
Founders' Prize reading period:
September 1 – October 31.

Address all correspondence to:

RHINO * P.O. Box 591
Evanston, Illinois 60204
Include SASE
or
editors@rhinopoetry.org

RHINO accepts electronic
submissions. Consult rhinopoetry.org
for details. For those submitting via
the postal service, please include
an SASE for response.

RHINO 2017 is available for $16
plus $3.50 for shipping & handling;
back issues are also available.
To order, visit our website,
or send check or money order
to the P.O. address.

RHINO is distributed for international retail sales
by IPG (Independent Publishers Group), ipgbook.com.

Our website features the Big Horn Blog, as well as
excerpts from past and current issues, events, audio
poems, poet interviews, and prize-winning
poems from our annual Editors' Prizes
and Founders' Prize Contest.
(See back cover for details.)
rhinopoetry.org

ISBN: 978-1-945000-010
ISSN: 1521-8414

© 2017, RHINO: The Poetry Forum, Inc.

All rights to material in this journal revert to
individual authors after *RHINO* publication.

EDITOR
Ralph Hamilton

SENIOR EDITORS
Virginia Bell
Deborah Nodler Rosen
Angela Narciso Torres

ASSOCIATE EDITORS
Lisa Croneberg
Carol Eding
Gail Goepfert
Ann Hudson
Matt Kelsey
Beth McDermott
Kenyatta Rogers
Jacob Saenz
Valerie Wallace

MANAGING EDITORS
Jan Bottiglieri
David Jones

ASSISTANT EDITORS
Kelsey Hoff
Christine Martin
Bethany Mueller

OUTREACH EDITORS
Noelle de Jesus (for translations)
Tim McLaughlin (for *40 Readings in 40 Cities*)

EDITORIAL ASSISTANT
Rochelle Jones

WEBMASTERS
Matt Kelsey
Valerie Wallace

INTERNS
Johanna Jimenez
Emily Johnson
Frani O'Toole
Margaret Saigh

ADVISORY BOARD
Michael Anderson
Enid Baron
Paulette Beete
YZ Chin
Alice George
Chris Green
Deborah Nall
Julie Parson-Nesbitt

CREDITS
Design by David Syrek
Illustrations by Albert Richardson
Back cover illustration by Tom Bachtell
Page number ornament by David Lee Csicsko
Production by Godfrey Carmona

CONTENTS

Editors' Note	x	
Editors' Prizes	xii	
Founders' Prize	xiv	
Samuel Ace	*The moon just hidden*	1
Irene Adler	*White Hyacinths*	3
Anna Akhmatova	*Cinque* translated from the Russian by Don Mager	4
Jessica Guzman Alderman	*By Saying One Thing We Exclude Another*	7
Catherine Allen	*Moonrise Departure, High Andes*	8
Steven Alvarez	*yr Polis B contracts & opening for a minute*	9
John Amen	*My Gallery Days, 16*	11
Majeed Amjad	*Ghazal* translated from the Urdu by Shiza Sophia Sabir	12
Dostena Anguelova	*Three and Something Deaths* translated from the Bulgarian by Holly Karapetkova	13
José Angel Araguz	*Fruit King*	14
Shauna Barbosa	*Something African with a K*	15
Sarah Bates	*Every Morning I Used to Bury the Wind*	16
Jake Bauer	*If You Seek a Pleasant Peninsula*	17
Jeanne Marie Beaumont	*Do you like candy, dearie?*	18
Abigail Beckel	*Pucker and Squint*	19
Deborah Bernhardt	*I Saw the Corridor*	20
Mary Block	*The Mosquito Bite*	21
Silvia Bonilla	*Bone Harp*	22
Jude Brancheau	*Suicide Ride*	23
Mark Brazaitis	*Depression, the Sit-Com*	24
Jay Brecker	*Looking Glass*	25
Gaylord Brewer	*Last Sunday Afternoon Before You Leave a Good Place to which You'll Never Return*	26
Matthew Burns	*Five Practical Posthumous Uses for Human Bones*	27
CR Callahan	*Pet Shop*	28
Lauren Camp	*Today and Other Flowers*	30
Chris Campanioni	*To be named*	32
Kayleb Rae Candrilli	*Making the Desert Wet*	34
John Randolph Carter	*Over There*	35
Andrés Cerpa	*At the Tree Line* *Like Sleep to the Freezing*	36 39
Leila Chatti	*Reciting Poetry in the Psychiatric Ward*	41
Nina Li Coomes	*Hiroshima is a city of light.*	43

Tommy D'Addario	*Anniversary*	45
Kristina Marie Darling	*The Sadness of Small Houses*	46
Peter Davis	*The Dainty Ninjas*	47
	My Love For You	48
Adam Day	*Which Is to Say*	49
Nandini Dhar	*The Fortnightly Doll Funeral*	50
Emari DiGiorgio	*Disappearing Lady*	51
Colin Dodds	From *Crossing Bedford Avenue*	52
Ronald Dzerigian	*Dream of Light and Space Debris*	56
Meg Eden	*chiang mai love poem*	58
Florbela Espanca	*Vain Desires*	60
	translated from the Portuguese by Carlo Matos	
Naoko Fujimoto	*Enough Is Never*	61
Michael Joseph Garza	*Beacon*	62
Ellen Goldsmith	*Shavings*	64
Lola Haskins	*It*	65
	The Love Song of Frances Jane	66
Sara Henning	*Disassociation Aubade*	67
Andrea Hollander	*"Mind Is East Hidden by Trees"*	68
Michael Homolka	*Rhapsody with Fever*	69
Kathryn Hunt	*Ursa Major Prowls the Chugach Range*	70
Rochelle Hurt	*Middling*	71
	The Incorruptible Head of St. Catherine of Siena	72
Safia Jama	*Oil Miniature in a Bone Frame*	74
Willie James	*Andrew Wyeth: Helga*	75
Brionne Janae	*Naked Pizza Friday*	78
Lesley Jenike	*Black Heart*	79
Joe Jiménez	*A pencil and a bowlful of pears.*	81
Erin Jones	*Dream Him Dead*	83
Jason Joyce	*Succulents*	84
Kendra Langdon Juskus	*How to Die in Peru*	85
Leah Claire Kaminski	*After Reading James Wright*	87
Kara Krewer	*Human Eyes*	89
Peter Krumbach	*The Duck*	90
Arden Levine	*Cake*	91
Jeffrey Little	*Lost King Forward*	93
Ginna Luck	*The Problem With Grief Is That It Never Lets Me…*	94
Cody Lumpkin	*Heavy Winter Coat*	95

CONTENTS

DM Macormic	Now That His Husband Is Gone, He Wears Only Dresses	96
Lauren Mallett	Requiem for an Unseeable Gravity	98
Cynthia Manick	Southern Impression	99
Gail Martin	Just When We Are Lost	100
Brooke McKinney	Killing the Leaves	101
Rachel Mennies	Removing Him from the Sex Scenes in All of Your Books	102
Faisal Mohyuddin	Partition, and Then	104
Carolyn Moore	Dear John Letter	105
Jennifer Moss	A Spider Climbs A Thread and Sets its Web Aquiver	106
Benjamin Nash	The Wig	107
Erik Norbie	Marine Life Thrives in Unlikely Place: Offshore Oil Rigs	108
Olivia Olson	The Teacher in Town	109
Pablo Otavalo	Outside Utica	110
Eric Pankey	The Hyenas	111
Casey Patrick	AIR TEMPERATURE 82 AIR TEMPERATURE 82 CALM CALM SWELL	112
Milorad Pejić	Picking Up Baggage translated from the Bosnian by Omer Hadžiselimović	113
Seth Pennington	I Drive You Through Mosquito Truck Spray	114
Lizzy Petersen	Duration	116
Robbie Pock	Letter to a Danish Skeleton	117
Alison Prine	song of a small city Other People's Sadness	118 119
Doug Ramspeck	Revival	120
Rebekah Remington	Silverberry	121
Kylan Rice	Georgic, Tri-Cities	122
José Antonio Rodríguez	Plutonian Nights	125
Kathleen Rooney	L'invention Collective	126
Kristen Rouisse	Another Photograph of Appalachia	127
Leigh Camacho Rourks	For the Wife of Alexander Wood	128
Diane Schenker	Heimisch	130
Colin Schmidt	Mr. and Mrs. Armstrong	131
JD Scott	Variations on an Attachment to	132
Peter Sears	My Bigfoot Newsletter	134

Jacquelyn Shah	—Qself, Jading	135
Yudit Shahar	Anew	136
	translated from the Hebrew by Aviya Kushner	
Lee Sharkey	Spellbound	137
Alix Anne Shaw	Never Again an August Paradise	138
	Truth operations / The most real day	139
Kevin Simmonds	Exit Wound	140
Brian Simoneau	Three-Year-Old Makes the Visiting Poet's Portrait	143
Joannie Stangeland	Gazebo	144
Joyce Sutphen	Reading Anna Swir in October	145
Jason Tandon	April Foolishness	146
John Allen Taylor	Monster	147
Casey Thayer	Chucky Be Drowning	148
	Metamorphosis with Drainage Pipe and Playboy	150
Robert Thomas	Sonnet with Schlock and Yonder	152
Z.G. Tomaszewski	Chronicle	153
Sarah Viren	A Dialogue With Translation	154
David Welch	The Afterlife	156
Joshua Marie Wilkinson	That's Where Both of You Were When I Slept	157
Mary-Sherman Willis	The Plot	158
Tim Wood	Shiki	159
Jan Worth-Nelson	House Hunting	162
Shana Youngdahl	Week 2	163
	Week 4	164
Theodora Ziolkowski	Girlhood Decorum	165

Contributors' Notes	169
Donors	184
Founders' Prize Information	inside back cover

EDITORS' NOTE

All I have is a voice
To undo the folded lie

wrote W. H. Auden in his poem, "September 1939." That is poetry's meager gift, and yet also its enormous power: to reveal the realities of how our lives, our hopes, and our illusions are lived out, both inwardly and outwardly. As James Baldwin observed, "The poets [are] the only people who know the truth about us."

Now in our 41st year, the poems in *RHINO 2017* reflect the uncertain times in which we live—the doubts and dread, as well as the heady courage, fierce resolve, subversive humor, and buoyant faith in the future. But even more, they provide stunning evidence of poets' ability to transform first-hand, fearless discernment into revelatory art.

Our poets explore both the world as they find it, along with their own minds' anxious imaginings:

Reconstruct the reef: the staghorn, / bottlebrush, cat's paw, cluster coral— / and the underwater glow the moon / coaxed from the latticework undergirding.
Casey Thayer

The capital burns on the horizon, tumbles into a chasm between land and land.
Lee Sharkey

A pair of hyenas stood at the door, dressed not unlike missionaries: black pants, / white button down shirts, their backpacks a little too snug under their armpits.
Eric Pankey

We take shelter in dead cows and / lift ourselves with hooks to keep out of sight. / At checkpoints, our dangling bodies / hold legs to chest, as instructed, to avoid detention.
Silvia Bonilla

Other poems express the existential doubts that stalk and taunt:

I check my teeth in a knife's reflection. / Or maybe I am looking behind me / quick as a silverfish (gross) / to see if I can sleuth the heartquake / happening in my chest. / As usual, there is nothing there.
Abigail Beckel

And what about the question mark that follows / you along the city streets, across gum-spotted / sidewalks, over puddled gutters, daily shadow
Jeanne Marie Beaumont

Maybe hammers. Maybe / ice under the cliff's orange rock // reaching down toward the earth. / Maybe nothing. Maybe nowhere.
David Welch

Yet our poets' work also shimmers with courage, and beauty, and wisdom:

I saw the future with her clothes off // A Happy Meal-ness, sinking ship tingling / climbing the rope in gym class

Jason Joyce

I will not live any more in this / bowl as if I am something floating in soup. I will take only my feet, and my / stick because I am half-blind with this life and must tap my way. I will / climb to where the stone houses fade then break apart in the wind.

Lola Haskins

The truth about loneliness is it's lonely.

Joe Jiménez

God comes like that. Seven / seconds in Coltrane's Love that justify / the ways of love to man. Hardly ever / does it last that long.

Robert Thomas

The frog moon erupts from the Atlantic / & the fish begin to sing.

John Allen Taylor

I am creating myself anew / in simple words / asking gifts / from the gods of little mercies / asking not to surrender / to the evil words / that are born in darkness

Yudit Shahar

We who lose our way think / we have lost our home. / But no: home slowly, tightly, wraps itself around us.

Jennifer Moss

When President Kennedy declared, "when power corrupts, poetry cleanses," he was proclaiming poetry's capacity to convey complexity and contradiction, while unmasking the meretricious. Moreover, he was testifying to the singular power of truth-telling to foster the lasting habits of mind and spirit on which democracy depends.

"We all need witnesses," a friend once told me. She meant that we need sympathetic friends to help us decipher, challenge, and understand ourselves, our lives, and our world. The editors of *RHINO* are honored to share with you these poets and their poems: the best of companions.

Ralph Hamilton
for the Editors of *RHINO*

EDITORS' PRIZES 2017

FIRST PRIZE
At the Tree Line
by
Andrés Cerpa

SECOND PRIZE
Truth operations / The most real day
by
Alix Anne Shaw

HONORABLE MENTION
Letter to a Danish Skeleton
by
Robbie Pock

TRANSLATION PRIZE
Picking Up Baggage
by
Milorad Pejić
translated from the Bosnian by Omer Hadžiselimović

FOUNDERS' PRIZE 2017

FIRST PRIZE
Exit Wound
by
Kevin Simmonds

RUNNERS-UP
Andrew Wyeth: Helga
by
Willie James

Shiki
by
Tim Wood

In addition, we selected contest poems by the following poets for publication in this issue of *RHINO*:

Samuel Ace	Leah Claire Kaminski
Jessica Guzman Alderman	Peter Krumbach
Sarah Bates	Brooke McKinney
Mary Block	Rachel Mennies
Silvia Bonilla	Carolyn Moore
CR Callahan	Pablo Otavalo
John Randolph Carter	Seth Pennington
Leila Chatti	Diane Schenker
Meg Eden	Joyce Sutphen
Safia Jama	David Welch

Information on next year's contest can be found on the inside back cover and at rhinopoetry.org.

Samuel Ace

The moon just hidden
—for Maureen Seaton

December 31st 12:30:01 pm

The moon just hidden we soaked in the dawn on the steaming river and watched the mornings of grebes and herons ospreys and ravens the moon just hidden we walked into the woods without a map and found a town of foundations and roads under bits of snow a sift of shade in the corners looking out on the river a cradle held in red leaves a new year's court the moon just hidden we soaked in the steam a certain heel of knowledge all broken in tables and tarnish a stable of horses well fed and looking to hedge the traces of crying gulls then to soar with the green heron this time to touch an old friend to take off my clothes and wonder at her wonder at my changed body my chest full of hair

The moon	the mornings
just hidden	of grebes
we soaked	a fountain
in the dawn	of fish
the moon	living under
steaming	the hot drain
the waters	the bits

Samuel Ace

of snow	soaked in the heart
in the shade	of the osprey
at the corners	on the far bank
of your mouth	the broken history
we looked	of horses
at the river	and restaurant
at the town	china just hidden
of hot mud	we were fed
we were held	with the traces
in a cradle	of gulls
of water beneath	the swift merganser
red leaves	and the curls
our new moon	of herons

Irene Adler

White Hyacinths

These white hyacinths I set beside
your stone could almost raise the dead.

Their scent is such a headiness
I think I hear bones stirring.

Maybe it's wrong to bring the sap of things
so near   risking whatever peace

was made here by a year's seasons.
But gesture is all now. Offerings.

And this is a field that none will reap
except the wind   hungry and sweeping.

Anna Akhmatova
translated from the Russian by Don Mager

Cinque

Beyond the cock-eyed waters, you write.
—Osip Mandelstam

I

As on a borderland of clouds
I recall your conversation,

And my conversation with you
When night stood as light as day.

How, ripped from the earth,
Aloft we soared like stars.

Neither despondency nor shame,
Not now, not later, not then.

But awake to actuality,
Hear how I invite you back.

And the door you left ajar,
I lack the will to seize and slam.

27 November 1945

II

Sounds decay into the ether,
And dark closes upon dusk.
In a forever unfeeling world
Two voices alone speak: yours, mine.
And under the wind from Lake Lagoda,
Invisible, a sound almost like bells,
Into splendid and lightly woven rainbows
The night's conversation was transformed.

1945. 20 Dec.

III

In bygone days I did not like
Anyone feeling sorry for me,
But with a drop of your pity
In my body I move like sunlight.
This is why, everywhere—dawn.
I move, and make miracles.
        This is why!

1945. 20 Dec.

IV

You know yourself, there is no peak of fame
For our meeting's bitter day.
What drop of memory is left for you?
My shade—what's a shade to you?
The dedication of a burnt drama,
From which there are no ashes?
Or stepping down from the frame
A New Year's fearsome portrait?
Or barely audible
The sound of birch coals,
Or what I did not write down
To finish the tale of another's affair?

1946. 6 Jan.

Anna Akhmatova

V

We had not breathed of heavy-lidded poppies
Yet, nor yet known our guilt.
But what did our stars already know
Of the heartache for which we were born?—
And what invisible glow
Had joined our minds in a single light?

1946. 11 Jan.

Note: *This poem was written for Isaiah Berlin (1909-1997), an English philosopher (born Jewish in Riga, raised in Petersburg, and became a British subject) who visited Akhmatova at the end of World War II.*

Jessica Guzman Alderman

By Saying One Thing We Exclude Another

Like the dog crushes the bone in her jaw.
Like the charm slips from its chain, catches
a pocket. Returning to that apartment
nine months after his death to find the cactus
split at the neck, clay pot scattered into continents;
birthday cake on a compass—crumbs disrupt
the dead ants huddled against the baseboards.
What soothsaying did you expect? To find
a honeycombed t-shirt and then the moth
trapped in a candle's wax. Only this sward
slivered by the window, where a mushroom
stretches its crooked stem above the grass,
sunlight snagged on the scales of its cap.

Catherine Allen

Moonrise Departure, High Andes

Mist followed moon rising
filled mountain crevices
like milk.

"Mother Moon,"
you said.
"Moon Day."

Mist followed moon rising
like unspun wool
trailing from spindles.

"Moon Day,"
you said.
I wept.

Your old hard hand
light as mist
brushed back my hair.

Note: *In the Quechua language a clear night of full moon is called* <u>*killa p'unchay*</u>, *"moon day."*

Steven Alvarez

yr Polis B contracts & opening for a minute

9:05 there are days when data are not ready for harvest
9:08 & that's one more day w no income
9:11 & can a crew leader Polis B workers to this camp apollo slamming Polis A
9:16 where they worked five weeks polling karma & picking green data
9:22 & when the fields of his trip to east & west Polis A trucks & buses
9:26 again will not
9:37 decisions
9:39 outside of normal
9:42 twenty thousand Polis B migrants are ferried to the fertile fields of Polis A
9:45 virginity eastern shores of Polis B for carbon chips uranium
9:49 & potatoes
9:59 for one Polis B crew
10:01 hardship climaxed disaster
10:03 death of a Polis B migrant
10:05 we haven't really wrote abt
10:12 Polis A parliament through it
10:15 for you
10:16 predecessor ever happened before w any Polis B crews coming up north
10:22 entry level
10:25 thank you
10:27 every year as predictable as the seasons
10:30 there are accidents resulting in death & serious injury to these labels
10:35 on june six nineteen fifty seven
10:38 at the intersection of Polis A troops we all went to Polis A highway one or
10:42 two nine miles from Polis B
10:46 twenty-one Polis B migrants were killed
10:49 three females
10:50 & the baby boy
10:52 the Polis A police report
10:53 stated one of the causes on the high loss of life was the
10:57 packaging of the occupants of
11:02 tax cuts are the Polis A

Steven Alvarez

11:04 three hundred migrants live in this Polis B camp owned & operated by
11:08 Polis A association of Polis A
11:14 this is my great housing
11:15 ninety miles from Polis C
11:51 knowledges november the last of the labor
11:55 buses & cards
11:57 approach the southern polis
11:58 to start the cycle all over again
12:10 for gold & the glory of god

John Amen

My Gallery Days, 16

I lived like an anchorite on the lee side of kink,
Sigur Rós, Zarathustra & Kierkegaard's leap,
libido on a binge & o yea Allison's genius grant.

    —her residency in Baltimore,
    & how many times did I peddle blood
    to satirize my family's provincialism?

    Accuse her all you like of imitation,
she defended her "Red & Green Docks of Reeding"
    all the way to the Whitney in September.

    O come on, you remember Allison;
    she's ash now on 109th—others did worse,
ventriloquists on forever methadone, their abstracts

sold for change @ yard sales in Bellmore & Syosset,
    the years pass like nodding on Coney Island.

Majeed Amjad
translated from the Urdu by Shiza Sophia Sabir

Ghazal

The roadside is the scent of scattered roses
All hues: red, vermilion, purple roses

On the horizon, the fog of all time
Songs, rivulets, winged life, butterflies, roses

Fully absorbed in her embroidery, sews
The rose-bride on the rose-world's robe – roses

From the world of lachrymose dew, proud,
They're walking by, flashing smiles, those roses

See my torn robe-side and see the cowl of spring,
Here sprinkled stains of wine, over there – roses!

To give color to that flower face
Braided up in her curls – roses!

The thoughts of a lover are chain-linked tipsy seasons,
And the loved one's beauty: a glimmer of roses

My eyes take each turn of the time signals as
A wave of blood, black smoke of the hearts, roses

Catching fire, just half-lit, silently laughing
Like the prophets' radiant faces – roses!

What talisman is this? Whose hand is behind
This world within a world – of roses!

My life was but spent mourning for the loss of spring
Let them bloom on my grave, forever – the roses!

Dostena Anguelova
translated from the Bulgarian by Holly Karapetkova

Three and Something Deaths

With what boredom the trees are blooming
besieged with green.

All the leaves and the branches are present
(salt drizzles from the loose knit of the sky)
filling the gardens
where death and winter
loved to laze around—
naked dogs, their legs turning blue.

Now it rains, but the souls of the trees
are turning into ravens—
three and something deaths
separate them from my childhood.

José Angel Araguz

Fruit King

My aunt cut through
the Fruit King easy,
knowing by sight
what was ripe,
what good. The King
would smile
his cartoon smile
from his sign
as she considered
unblinking pears,
flushed mangoes,
the bated breath
of oranges. Her hands
would pass
and halt,
two birds,
not in any hurry.
Her fingertips, amused,
would linger, peck.
To me, a child
prone to singing
himself down the aisles
until my aunt's hands ruffled
and pinched me
back to silence,
the fruit appeared
to be making every
effort to hold still,
a light on their skin –
she could have been the moon.

Shauna Barbosa

Something African with a K

In Virginia, years after, you got into gardening. Because you had lost your hair, you wanted to watch things grow. The baby you almost had would have set the table. You like to think of a girl because Tony said on the trolley back to his house that he would want to name her after his mother. But you thought her name was ugly. Despite your father being African, you thought the name was too African. But you love its American meaning. You never once cooked for Tony in the dirty apartment overlooking the Boston skyline he shared with his brother. You think the baby would have been this tall girl who set the table, a girl named after her grandmother. Koshi. Kochi. Koshie. A silent letter anywhere, but you don't remember because you said no. You said you would call her Grace.

Sarah Bates

Every Morning I Used to Bury the Wind

I am sick of the rain that fell.

I killed that man. I wash my sheets
every morning and watch Pat Sajak
and honeysuckle spin. I bury
hemlocks into my palms
when my mother says
it was a bad dream.

I burn the whole earth
into my right shoulder.
I retrace my steps in the front yard
to heal my knuckles
to the throat
of a man
who believed my body
was only meant
for listening to the wind.

It's how he rowed
across my fields,
ate his eggs over easy
the next morning.

How I searched my mother's jars
of grapevine for the old scent
of orchids,

but all I could remember
was how many bees
I'd killed that spring.

It's the way he dragged my clothes from the dryer
and I stopped thinking about God.

Jake Bauer

If You Seek a Pleasant Peninsula

Detroit Institute of Art, Kenneth Noland, Untitled, 1981:

> *The paper is the medium for these three prints. The color results from the fibers used to make the paper. The composition comes from molding the paper into horizontal bands by applying varying amounts of pressure to it.*

    The machine that applied the pressure
was bought from a woman in Watersmeet.
The pressure was sometimes like grabbing minnows
with her grandfather, other times like pushing
an owl through a tear in some fabric hung from
the clothesline. The woman's existence was the narrow
hall of the one-room library in that town. The yellows
of it. The lilac and alabaster. The wise old owl,
the more he knows, the less he says, he reminded
himself as he watched the woman under the jack pines
using her hands to talk to lovers, sometimes laying
them flat like rapids on the Ontonagon River, sometimes
making them judder like a camera, which, not too
long before had been invented, and, by pressing
down, also captured silent things.

Jeanne Marie Beaumont

Do you like candy, dearie?

And what about the question mark that follows
you along the city streets, across gum-spotted
   sidewalks, over puddled gutters, daily shadow,
      nightly stalker, an unwavering wavering,
cobra riled up—now a levitating specter, unsummoned
   ghost with a dowager's hump and monk's cowl,
      then the alliumatic steam rising off a cook pot,
curl from a film noir cigarette, or spry genie rubbed
   out of the period lamp who's eager to grant
      wishes if only you'd spin round, but you don't,
you won't look—it's too crooked to be trusted,
   perhaps some gust of fact or declaration will blow
      its top away, leave just the certifying point, but
till then you dash for blocks, run against lights, make
   quick turns where crowds thicken, wondering
      if you've shaken it at last, the way it sidles up,
sinuous unicyclist atop a nearly silent wheel—*shhh shhh*
   bending close by your ear to pose the question
      you're most loath to hear, and so you don't
listen, you'll never look, sensing its propensity to hover
   and to stick, to stir up uncertainty, pry open every box,
      all the while perfecting its impersonation of a hook.

Abigail Beckel

Pucker and Squint

The black spots on the sun are blooming.
NASA has discovered caves on the moon
that astronauts might be able to live in.
Too bad there aren't astronauts anymore.
I check my teeth in a knife's reflection.
Or maybe I am looking behind me
quick as a silverfish (gross)
to see if I can sleuth the heartquake
happening in my chest.
As usual, there is nothing there.
My blood muscle just keeps
beating fast as a double-dutch rope.
I am always seeing things
I wish I could make into reality.
Dutch scientists have now figured out
the basic properties of teleporting—
I can't wait to be particles beaming
from here to you. When the atoms
reconfigure, I'll be a little different,
my hair a shade darker, a few memories
gone, the hollow of my shoulder deeper
than you remember. The old me
will niggle at your mind, tease you.
I will haunt you like a hummingbird,
always darting away in the corner
of your eye, wondering who you love more.
Good thing I'm worrying about this now
so I'll be ready for beam-me-up day,
the future me and you. The knife fogs,
everything behind me is pucker
and squint. And there's the past,
steadfast, steadfast, steadfast.

Deborah Bernhardt

I Saw the Corridor

bodies with anecdotes begin in a national airport the early days of Homeland a same-day ticket triggering the Special Search I said *please* but it was not like "The Race" which I read to every Intro class because of that line break goodbye line break to my body my searcher upped his diligence when I said please then both of us very quiet but as he zipped my bag shut he said which airline, that way, run, which is a lot like the Sharon Olds poem bet I sprint as fast or faster than Sharon Olds false alarm of course

the next trip a continuum

landed then economy car the whole smiley thing about upgrading to a four door the whole scare you thing about arsenal of rental insurance so I go *my grandfather is dying give me the keys* procedure sped up a bit Pop-pop still lucid asked how I got there

ha not a lot else to say

did not know him well we did death alone just Pop-pop and I at Veteran's for three days then I did hearing is the last sense to go on day three I bothered to wash my hair in the visitor's sink but why bother I was there

Mary Block

The Mosquito Bite

I said, trust me like the little dog has to,
having been so denatured. Having so little
to do with a wolf. Follow me
and make a home where the weather hums,
where the leaves grow monster-wide.
In a city slipping, feet-first, into the sea.
Like you I put my faith in larvicide and lizards,
in the tongues of frogs. I built a house
from salt and fossil shells.

Outside the bullfrog sings for his bride,
for the mouse and the limp-tailed rat.
The tail of a cat or some animal flicks
at the slats of our bedroom window.

I told our boy, in so many words, the fate of foxes.
I told him the tree frog is a friend—
that even poison has its place.
But still he woke with a red ring rising
from his side.

A ring of roses is either an amulet
or a nothing. Either way
I hung a wreath outside our door.
I said trust me like the little dog has to.
Trust me, son, to be the mother
that all soft animals require
and the little dog laughed.

Silvia Bonilla

Bone Harp

We take shelter in dead cows and
lift ourselves with hooks to keep out of sight.
At check points, our dangling bodies
hold legs to chest, as instructed, to avoid detention.
All language snuffed out
by the blue perch of meat. It's a miraculous
thing to be wrapped in it.
After we pass, relief rustles
the epidermis—enough to warm us
for some time.
Who trained our bodies for this?
Poverty is violence.
We know the look of dead
things behind pinned drapes and how to make
history in one day. We bent at the knees
to kiss our children's faces.

Jude Brancheau

Suicide Ride

Head pushed against the measure
and just tall enough to enter, I had to go on

the rattling Runaway Mine Train, wait
in the maze of the line, that back and forth,

see the same old strangers passing
over and over again—like the bunch dad could tell,

turning my head like a knob to their tats,
also fought in the war and *need a bath*—

the same ones bouncing around
in front of us, reaching for beams in jungles

of angles beneath the higher tracks—
me taking the jerks and twists *like a man*

and keeping my eyes open by reading a back
of Cheap Trick tour dates—and dad screamed

his laughs, was some crazy stranger way out
of his seat, showing off his surrender.

Mark Brazaitis

Depression, the Sit-Com

Every week, the hero will try to kill himself
but fail in ever-more-comical ways:
by shooting his ear off;
by drinking poison that makes his face turn green
and gives him gas;
by jumping off the eighteenth story of a building
and into a truck-bed full of manure.
In earnest solidarity, people he knows well,
and people he barely knows,
will share with him their problems,
a series of inane calamities:
a cake over-baked,
a broken coffee cup—a favorite!—
a lost gerbil,
each punctuated by laughter
from a laugh track.
They will follow with their homemade remedies
to heal the horror in his head and heart:
"Jumping jacks—a hundred a day."
"Bananas are soothing. They'll help you sleep."
"Underwater meditation. Guaranteed."
His psychiatrist, with a beard and glasses
and the requisite gallows humor,
will dash off a prescription with a warning:
"This may work—but only after six weeks.
I wish patience came in a pill."

There will be a second season.
It will be a darker comedy,
although everyone will wear white.

Jay Brecker

Looking Glass

The glazier in our town has twin daughters, identical in almost every way. Except one you can see through, one you can see into. People being what they are rarely notice the difference. They see what they see. What passes in front of them is expected. Some see a mirror. Others see a window. Each sister, though, when looking at the other sees her own disappearance.

Gaylord Brewer

Last Sunday Afternoon Before You Leave a Good Place to which You'll Never Return

The sky still tender from night's berating
wind, the gate slouched from the beating
it took and didn't deserve. That sort of thing.
Church bell stupidly determined on
the lengthening hours, and the chickens,
who shit the same on Sunday as every other,
whose scripture is food—hard bread, soft cabbage,
broken corn if they can get it.

No nod to the world's depredations,
no exhausting despair, nothing at all, not here,
of the calamity of love. No quick gestures
with the hands. Maybe just a single
image of a woman unmoving on a swing,
the headlights of a car that may never arrive.
Maybe a spell of wildflowers, tentatively identified
from the pocket where they died:
spotted rockrose, dusky dog-fennel, sage.
Pimpernel, cistus, and marigold.
But too you could have all the names wrong,
so maybe not even that, not even.

Matthew Burns

Five Practical Posthumous Uses for Human Bones

1.
Phalanges, twenty, bleached: line the white mantle in winter, candelabra of memory and loss, gone fingers pointing up to a sky as unconcerned as dirt. Picket fence, tiny pikes upon which you impale everything unsaid.

2.
Polished radius: weaker side, engrained with antipathy: shaped and sharpened: a bread knife or scythe. Grain of field, grain of bone. An arm to reach out and reap and bring toward some feast. Hunger will never cease, and we need to eat.

3.
Sternum (shorn of ribs): doubtless: axehead/maul. Guard of heart for hardwood to be split—black birch, bur oak, something that burns long and hot. Shape a handle of hickory; hone and lash tight before the first strike.

4.
Right patella: paperweight for utility bills, bundled junk, anything to be ground into soil.

5.
Hyoid, broken, crushed, gilded: necklace, raw gold chain, worn slightly higher on the neck than comfortable: jaw beneath jaw, tacit mandible. Ghost of some gone voice healed after six weeks of silence. Tie just tight enough to bite into the throat's fine skin, to remember to speak again.

CR Callahan

Pet Shop

There weren't many no's
in that Rikki-Tikki-Tavi childhood
filled with creatures found in our jungle
behind the orange trees
or purchased with offering money
at the pet shop by our church.
God didn't miss the money
and we were unsupervised heretics
with air-holed containers
hidden in plain sight on the patio
by the bubbling aquarium and the bookcase
dusty with *Modern Classics*.
Our chihuahua lived in valid fear
of the boa constrictor
and our friends claimed the iguana
was a small dragon
fed on a diet of hibiscus blossoms
and fingertips.
We discovered the mortality of neglect
and had a corner near the back wall
where one had to be careful
when digging sad new graves.
Left to our own devices
we learned of possums, snakes, lizards
skunks, rats, mice, fish, dogs
and that forgiveness
is not available from the dead.
Our mother slept with the light on
eased shoes from the closet
with a hanger
stuffed towels beneath her door

and depended on us for rescue
when trapped on a toilet or chair or dresser.
We were he-men
our armor shining bright.
We hadn't yet learned how
to disappoint our women.

Lauren Camp

Today and Other Flowers

Today I sat with a woman who thinks without future.
Her house holds first and last things.
In a bowl, globes of grape, pale as elm leaves;
in another, a scatter of nuts that don't touch.
She eats like a prophet—first one, then the other.
Once she painted the undulant: threshed fields,
the thickening river two miles off.
Her brushes discovered the inside of landscape.
Now her skin's gone thin and violet, and her eyes hold caves.
She doesn't know me. What she doesn't know
isn't tragic. She's fallen through,
but her hands want to be moving. She sits
in her crowded house with two German shepherds.
She sits in her braces and blue pants with canes
by her side. Through the many tall windows,
she sees a sky drowning in blue.
Sees pines wrinkled in heat. It is afternoon,
and still is. Afternoon daisies.
From her I learn the koan of looking.
Open-throated Southwest pots—buff,
white and black—cluster in the kitchen.
She asks me a question studded with ending
and beginning; she's concentrating.
No deviation in the sheen of her thoughts.
She asks and repeats her question with the logic
of what's not important, with pieces
of asking. She's lived here for decades.
The days drift through her, and bloom into night.
She asks again where I'm going.
To the unfolding water, I tell her.
Her soft hands play with a purple pencil.

She does not latch her thoughts; she looks out
at the interior wall of the sky, the endless
distance. Together, we notice the birds that fly
to the feeder, their silent conversations
as they work on seed shells. This is why
we have shadow and yellow, why red-winged blackbirds,
why we have windows, why trees knot
at the river, and why the river turns around,
suddenly deciding to run off again
wherever its memory pleases.

Chris Campanioni

To be named

What a beautiful rite
        The before & not
Knowing a being
        Yet disclosed & neither
Clothed in any
        Thing other
Than flesh
        The lapel
Turned back &
        Meant to be
A continuation of
        The collar
Something
        Which binds
The throat
        I dream I was
Born without a face
        Or title &
Titled to only what
        Ever this body
Confluence &
        Each wave
Brings in
        The shore at dawn
Floridian pink
        Obelisk & I am in
The middle of this
        Ritual taken upon
The altar
        Marked & mark
Eted to fit

    Enduring versions of me
Shiver like
    A stone before
The mirror of
    Others & each camera
Eye recording
    Velvet tongue so
Sweet say anything
    You like consensual
Hallucinations the screen
    Of my interior
Which very few
    Will ever enter my
Deleted thoughts throat
    Without a tongue
City lights re
    Ceding but what beauty
To be named only
    At birth when I
Fell out & felt
    My new skin &
The sheen
    Of this turbulence
Trembling in
    Another's palms
& held up
    For others to
Look at & call
    Me what
You will

Kayleb Rae Candrilli

Making the Desert Wet
—after Hernan Bas' Laocoön's Sons

Before Christ what was there except dissonance, red ridges, and bison run in rhythm with one another? Because I am always lost, I tuck a vision of the last millennia into my breast pocket and it smokes up like black sand—the Pharaoh's Horses crushing my clavicle with bass heavy hooves. I'm always high on pesticides and saber tooth tigers because time isn't linear and death is one of the saints I pray to. If I were asked to say one true thing, I'd hold my breath through the ages. When I turn blue in the face, the desert becomes an ocean and I want you to imagine the cool insides of an abandoned conch shell. Run your fingers in and out of the smoothness and know my sex is just another illusion. Everything you thought you knew about me: mirage, and the tide all pulled back.

John Randolph Carter

Over There

Support hose threaten me with their urgency.
I bang my drum and leap in the air.
Columns of smoke rise beyond the distant hills.

A company of tired and forgotten soldiers
shuffles by, dragging dead ideals and aspirations
in frayed canvas bags.

The sun is white.
The sky is light blue.
The earth is bleached and pale.

Bored gunnery sergeants discuss azimuth headings
and windage as they pass.

I hide in the doorway, invisible in the blackness.
This is not my war.
I'm fighting with my underwear.

I wait till they are out of earshot and
then I leap in the air and bang my drum.

Andrés Cerpa

At the Tree Line

That year I rented a room without mirrors & smoked dope with my friends, alone, every chance I could get. The morning of my 22nd birthday, Bill pushed a bundle through the gap in my door & put two shots in our morning coffee. I went to work, read, got off early. Even though the house was empty there was always a palpable sense of return – slant soled shoes on the floorboards, whorls & piles of ash, a book laid open to its spine. Already dark, I watched a movie & called my father. His voice like thin smoke in blue light, while outside, the snow riddled the dark –

In art there is comfort, control & revision.
Iñárritu's *Biutiful* for example, where the son dies
& is met by his father, younger than him,

who offers safe passage & advice, a cigarette:
one last earthy comfort. In the tree line – fog, the sound
of the father's footsteps, the promise of the sea.

More likely, my father dies surrounded by the sterile
beep of suicidal green, tendered by the touch of a stranger
who will go home & outlive us both.

More likely, we are not met at the end. There are no words
or safe passage. Yet I, like you, can say whatever it is
I'd like to say about death. It is a vacant city

filling with birds. My father will meet me there.
The sins of this earth will be forgiven.
Maybe, death is too old to become tragic,

he's had his fun, has already slipped down oblivion's
staircase & still lies there, broken, looking up,
as the new gods saddle up & turn the hourglass over.

I will begin again, in my father's car –
the September he sat us down & told us
he would not die, but change.
The September when I asked
the simple questions of childhood,

plainly – he said, *This is what it does to you*,
the brakes clenched at a red light
outside of school, *Look:*

tremors: so many birds rising in unison
& without reason, mazed
in the rearview mirror, gone.

There is a current beneath us, a river
frozen as hell mimicking first the bare
branches, then sky. Whatever fear I choose,
the mirror, the shack of the mind
singed to the skyline, or drowning,
a thread like the broken stars
keeps hauling me back.

Tonight, I do not want to tell you my name
to hear it repeated. I want to scrape
my one chair to the middle of the room
& smoke alone with my burnt-to-shit coffee.

Andrés Cerpa

Maybe by morning I can walk outside

& watch my father's car glide to a stop.
Say, *Not today, Dad,*
I don't want to go, means, I want to go with you.

Andrés Cerpa

Like Sleep to the Freezing

Somewhere in summer my friends are burning through cane and cold beers in a 'twas heaven prayer card.

Between now and there I don't say much more than, How's the weather? to the rain.

It turns to snow.

Winter is the knife I carry but never use & we're dying but dying slow & that's life.

You scared?

I'm no longer sure my friends can save me.

But once I dreamt that death was a struggle for the last words you don't find, then you wake & everyone's there playing Wiffle ball again.

In the house we shared there was static & the trains shook the windows as they left.

I want to shake like that again.

The grass is always greener & the dead think so too, but they learn to let go.

I haven't.

My jacket's been stitched in dear Lord & late birdsong; in black branches & ice.

And my youth, I hold it, like a stovetop holds a blue flame, or how a child holds a revolver: guilty, thrilled in a black corner of the attic.

This is the brutal joy of moving closer to sleep.

Your head on the bar while we dance.

Andrés Cerpa

I'm walking through snow now, banished, not saying much & hoping I can become
like you: stripped of every decadence: light as the light on the floorboards.

Leila Chatti

Reciting Poetry in the Psychiatric Ward

Amidst all the blonde collegiate
nurses assigned to our wing, one
my mother's age who likes me.
She's sweet on my name—*same as Ali's
daughter!*—but calls me *sugar*, swallowing
the r, and winks one big dark
eye at me when I pass. Over the desk,
she leans in and says, like it's a secret, *I know
you're not crazy*, then laughs
because there's little else
she can do, can only shake her head and promise
to talk to the doctors. She's the only one
who believes me when I say
I teach poetry at the university—
claps her long-fingered hands and quotes
Maya Angelou, declares
herself a *phenomenal woman*, then adds
*and you're a little caged bird
singing*. When she asks me to
teach her about poetry, I am glad
for it—to stand by the nurses' station
with some semblance of use,
to punctuate the timeless stretch
of the ward with mini-lectures
on Brooks and Lorde and Hughes—
and on my last day, when it's determined
I can be trusted again
with my life, I am given
my things in a plastic bag
and she asks me

Leila Chatti

my favorite poem, I recite without thinking *won't you*
celebrate with me—and she smiles
as I'm led through the bolted doors
where she stands, waving, like a good host,
then says kindly *don't you ever*
come back now, you hear?

Nina Li Coomes

Hiroshima is a city of light.

1. the boxed back-and-forth of light & shade & light & shade & light & shade on the trolley from the train station, irreverent glimmers of sun on water reflected up from one of six rivers that feed the heart of the city the soft out of focus spotlight through screens in the hostel room a series of frilling lace cutouts between bare late December trees i had imagined it would be dark, weighty somehow, that the soil stained heavy with ash would reach fingers up into the buildings, thickening the air to a muddy crawl, little people veiled in shadows cast long and lasting on the pavement. but i was wrong, and Hiroshima was and is a city of light, even now, even still, even then

2. wood: partitioned. older than our grandmother with a clientele to match us wordlessly rolling our clothes into small bundles, pushed into the back of a shared locker, stepped into the baths, into the steam, the thick, a white robe clinging to our cheeks, making our hair twist in on itself and curl up into insincere half smiles, we wash our flesh suddenly lumbering sodden our welsh hips and german breasts the parts our father gave us, our round hands our round feet the slant of our mother's eyes an apology invisible under the mist, now, here, we are too big too much and then some, for this small space, for these small people, who scowl and stare and hem the air with their sighs, and why shouldn't they be, when we did this to them

3. what is the obligation of a body? the responsibility of a skeleton? how should one stand when sandwiched by war? the posture of both massacre and massacred? when love is made in an armistice, what color is the flag to be waved? is it salvation that is born, or simply the reality of a battle, the way fighting can sometimes look like fucking? is there mercy in the meeting? can a body apologise to itself? or forgive it?

4. keloid scars look like ambitious cobwebs. they stretch across skin in bumpy lumpy foaming strings, knotting and blanching across shoulder and bone, they are a braid of time or history something we ought not to carry underneath our pores but gets trapped there anyway, a resentful, muzzled bird, a swarm of flesh-locked bees, a school of jellyfish immobilized in plastic, the scar is stagnant but seems to seethe, somehow silent and humming at once and

Nina Li Coomes

5. she is covered with them, her face her arms her back her sagging breasts that float peacefully on the water's surface, the scar travels from the roots of her white hair as if even there her body is giving itself up to the Flash, the Bang, the Bomb and how it founded her in fires we cannot imagine, (but no one looks at her (because they are looking at us) so she must be a regular), unfathomably she swims towards us, her fire founded flesh crossing into our corner of the bath, confused guilt rising in greasy clouds, we are sorry we are sorry we are sorry our half-american bodies are so sorry but she pushes the apologies away with a spider-webbed hand, sends them skittering across the pool into a tiled corner, she smiles at us, she inclines her head, she extends us grace in an evening greeting, her body an altar we cannot deserve, grace like a halo, a lantern, a bobbing glow in a city awash with light

Tommy D'Addario

Anniversary

A man and a child go where the water meets the sand,
where the water meets also the air, and the gulls who slip

the seam between all three. And the gulls are cotton
snared among the dune grass, or they are kites cut loose

into the air, or they are buoys bobbing out to sea. And the child
points at the gulls and cannot take the point back,

and runs among the gulls, who slip the seam between
the child and the clouds, who cannot take the winds

back. The child names the clouds and cannot take
the names back, and lies face-up to watch them pass.

The man breathes it all in and tastes salt, and with the salt
he remembers, and he cannot take the remembering back,

just as he loves the child and cannot take the love
back, and slips the seam between the two.

Kristina Marie Darling

The Sadness of Small Houses

The other wife is always present, counting the buttons down the back of my neck. Husband, you know the coldness of her hands. The break in her voice. Her stop and start.

When the diamond is kept in a separate box from the ring itself, its theft remains a perpetual possibility, but on most days an abstraction.

From the *balcons*, she must have been beautiful: white on white on white.

When will they unlock the door. The violence of a room is in its plainness. The dark cloths on the arms of the chairs. The stutter of new foliage against the glass.

Husband, you know the sound a dish makes when it shatters.

When I say your name, the women—one by one—
                                      stop breathing

Peter Davis

The Dainty Ninjas

They are more beautiful and
predictable than the massive
ninjas, who are not predictable
or beautiful, but like wisps
of horse hair, you find them
in your imagination, stirred
in a past silent sauce.
My advice isn't very helpful
but I'd advise you to get
help somewhere. The dainty
ninjas, like boarded up ghosts,
hop on one foot, trying
to see the thunderstorm.
These ninjas aren't powerful
but they are merciful, like
a god that no religion has
discovered yet.

Peter Davis

My Love For You

First you feel a sort of nagging in your knees,
like a curly bug is crawling up your leg.
Before you can swipe it away, it's gone, cast backward
into the wind like the look on Lot's wife's face.
Speaking of salt, my love jumps through
the flavor of your dinner and impresses you
with the tanginess of sorrow.
When you want to open up and swallow,
it turns out you can't connect the food to your pie-hole.
Everyone's pie-hole is someplace different.
For instance, mine is in my hand and when I
wave I'm showing the world where I
load the insides. During a handshake, my lips
are closed but the moment I let go, they open
into a scream that sounds a lot like a tired
vacuum cleaner. I wish my love were better
but it's worse. I'm like a prince who turns
into a frog. Or, rather, like a prince who
isn't a prince or a frog, just some local hick
who's finally come around to the big cities
of Shit Sucks and O Fuck. Where the national
anthem is "I've Fallen and I Can't Get Up."

Adam Day

Which Is to Say

My parents blessed my birth
        with celibacy. An ordinary

and anxious child; I have never
        been comfortable underground.

Though I was a member
        of the Socialist Party for a time,

initially to meet women
        as liberal with their bodies

as with their politics. Eventually,
        I embraced Marxism, which is to say

I had lingering doubts
        about my masculinity. Ordinariness

has become something
        to pursue. In future years

I will be kept from falling
        from high places by a sense of responsibility

to loved ones that will fade
        into routine. I will become obese

and a dedicated philanderer—my excess
        hiding, like god, the tool of my degradation.

Nandini Dhar

The Fortnightly Doll Funeral

A window in a room is a form of atonement, Mother says.
An atonement against the impenetrability of the bricks,

the cement that keeps the house together. Father never cuts
the grass in the courtyard; the abundance of wildflower red,

holocaust orange. Inside, the house-snake has laid its eggs.
From our corner near the window, we can hear

the snake-mother breathing. Our aunt stands behind
the door, wiping off the sweet crust of milk and sugar

from the baby's lips. Baby does not wriggle its fingers.
Baby is a porcelain doll with the face of our aunt's father,

closes its eyes when one pushes back its head. Black
eyelashes like arrowheads. This is the twenty-third

baby we have buried inside our home in the last eleven
months. Aunt keeps pushing them out of her belly.

Although, none of them ever learns to cry. No one
cares about finding them a coffin. Grandmother digs

a hole inside the kitchen floor with her shovel and axe,
Mother throws the babies in. Uncles clap. Aunt blinks,

we're ordered to dance around the hole holding hands.
We do, singing *Ring-a-ring-a-roses* at the tops

of our voices. This is a song that Aunt taught us.
Aunt was a school marm, before all she wanted

to do was to have babies to play with.

Emari DiGiorgio

Disappearing Lady

To run from the everyday collapse,
its chain-link and water torture tank.
A woman like a wisp of cloud, lunula

of nail. She halves herself again.
If a black hole is a dead star,
how does it die? For her next trick,

balanced on ice pick—a bag of flour
to cake. No yellow wallpaper here.
She's a stitch of floss, drawing blood.

The unpaved road, dirt lot. The same
dream on hands and knees. A contortion
gone wrong: trying to hang herself

with her own hair. This woman can fit
so many things between her legs. Hurry.
We all die so slowly, then all at once.

Colin Dodds

From Crossing Bedford Avenue
—*for Harry Essex*

Hate
is the only way to comprehend some things

Your body was found Tuesday off Bedford Avenue
It was no surprise
It was sooner or later

The prophesies all end in apologies and Bedford Avenue
wins a ghost to malinger among skateboarding financiers
food fetishists, cultural careerists, the falsely disheveled
heirs to deepening trouble kissing the ass of an angry algorithm—
all the feckless little fucks too craven to get themselves killed

Hate is the only language

Oh friend
and miserable shade who stole my friend
This will admit no contradiction
I love you and hate
you who has taken you from me

Oh friend playing basketball at three am on summer nights
beside the Aztec ruin of McCarren Pool
Wandering rubbled East River piers
Watching Orson Welles' *The Trial* all rainy afternoon
before a night of big beers and brave young women
at Rosemary's

Oh friend who did what no one else did or would
Drawing the sephirothic tree with kielbasa slices in a pan
Reenacting *Who's On First* with your pet turtle
Rubbing vomit into cheap landlord carpet
while every surface clicked open onto busy infinity
Reeling around that tiny apartment
like it was a sacred grove roaring out *Finnegan's Wake*

And now you've gone and followed the gone
        Gone the long afternoons of unhindered speculation
        Gone the Avenue A cafe with a bathtub full of broken computers
        Gone the wobbly tables bracketed by the wild-eyed dispossessed and messianic, with every mystery school cracked open just in time for everyone to be totally on their own
        Gone the dense dirty laissez-faire summer streets dotted with cheap-drink elephant graveyards
        Gone the mystical atheists scratching at the edges of a locked room
        Gone the hippie holdouts techno-anarchists misanthropes with no natural or spiritual homes
        Gone the early evenings when visits to the record store became visits to the liquor store
        Gone the sunken sofas of self-proclaimed prophets and scavenging squatters identically incensed and grasping for a quantum loophole or a historical-dialectic excuse, invoking Gurdjieff Tesla and Wilhelm Reich to bludgeon or just comprehend their own neglect and isolation
        All of them feeding but not growing, fermenting into something else
                The beer of the stars you said
        Time's truants, Hart Crane might've called them
        Citizens of the universe

Colin Dodds

You made a break
to the clear light the Coors Light
to your decade-long public suicide on Bedford Avenue
dim now like a stale wound

					* * *

In a heat wave, you crossed Bedford Avenue
a final time asking beer money from street vendors
And on North Sixth Street beside a thrice-failed café
with nowhere to retire to,
you retired nonetheless

After a suicide we all go on trial
forced to reopen negotiations
with the inconsistent thing that sustains us

On that last corner a week later you've boiled down
to deli flowers votive candle framed photo
and a piece of red scrap metal
covered in misspelled Magic Marker wishes
More flotsam on the swelling tide of a mental health
that could choke a good man
and often does

Past streets of investment-colored condos
a lone wooden piling emerges from the calm river
just beyond the reach of the new pedestrian pier's clean concrete
and stainless steel rails

All around, tender territories languish
and liquidate with the last of the margins
where once we might have lived

No longer the rough refuge of ill-employed refuseniks
No longer the thrift-store bargain bin of reinvented wheels
Bedford Avenue overflows
Its citizens willing
citizens of something smaller

       Oh friend
retired from friendship
retired from all this
and friend
who murdered my friend

May my thoughts
climb the sunlight
to where you are
and reach them
in whose care you have arrived
whom I can not instruct
but only ask
to close your eyes
and open them again

Ronald Dzerigian

Dream of Light and Space Debris
—*after reading* Searching for the International Space Station, *by Sean Patrick Kinneen*

A stack of books, a ceramic walrus on top, a plant
—tips dry—in a white vase on a glass-topped burl

wood side table. My wife sleeps on the couch, feet
wrapped in a knitted throw; I watch her from

my chair. Her eyes turn beneath their lids; perhaps
her dreams consider the colors of light through blinds—

our two girls sleep silently. Clock ticks; the ceiling
fan sounds like draining water. I've just read a poem

about a space station. It is moving; people are inside
turning knobs, eating, sleeping, weightless. A stack

of books would come apart in the heavens; light
is different without dust and rusted beams parting

plumes of atmosphere. Sleep pulls us through clouds
of memory—we forget who we are when we sleep.

Our youngest wakes us and we don't ask her to recall
the bad dream; it will be forgotten. My wife's face

moves against soft folds of woven pink, brown,
yellow, orange, waking without waking. The ceiling

fan sounds like water; the station remains above us;
our stack of books will not come apart mid-air.

I see the photograph of the one person bruised
by a meteorite, Ann Hodges—Sylacauga, Alabama—

struck in 1954 while napping on her couch. I think
of flames that rise from surfaces that cut across the sky,

lines ignited red or green. I consider the inability
to fall; the orbit of bodies that shine back as we look up.

Meg Eden

chiang mai love poem

the ladyboy jumps into our songtaew

battered feet in heels too small

wig tilted, false flower falling from her hair

underneath: her throbbing adam's apple.

what I remember most clearly: her hairy legs, scalded

from the knee down

as if someone rolled her through a parking lot of bike mufflers

& the ends of her skirt burned as if bitten.

she holds up her fingers, fat like bananas with callouses

she talks like any girl: *please, kha. no money, kha. just need to go a few blocks, kha.*

& all I can think to ask her is: *how did you get in our taxi without money?*

she presses for a stop & jumps over the back of the truck bed

into the pitch black Thailand night.

what about the burns on her legs? won't they get

infected in this elephant heat, bare

in a mosquito city sky—

he is so she is so bare

with love, she will be eaten raw by fire

for love, I am still afraid of the idea

of being touched by a man.

Florbela Espanca
translated from the Portuguese by Carlo Matos

Vain Desires

I wanted to be the sea's proud bearing,
laughing and singing vast expanses.
I wanted to be a stone, unthinking,
a stone path, rude and strong.

I wanted to be the sun's immense light,
humble and good and without ill will.
I wanted to be a tree, rough and dense,
mocking the vain world and even death.

But the sea also sorrows...
and trees pray,
opening their arms to heaven like believers.

And the haughty and powerful sun, after one day,
cries bloody tears in its agony.
And the stones... those... they tread down everyone...

Naoko Fujimoto

Enough Is Never

"I will take the trash out," he says.
The door closes in a small house.

Our hearts, like rhubarbs,
liquidate in a garbage disposal.

Magpies bring pieces from the glass company
adding more stones to the riverbank.

I glue my deodorant in his cabinet
because enough is never enough.

Hair upholsters my eyes on his sheets.
"Orange toenails," he says.

I slip my feet under his thighs.

We hear her lively laugh—
a neighborhood girl raises her sunglasses

with freckles on her clavicles,
her white dress flares.

Michael Joseph Garza

Beacon

why kill a moth
enamored with proton
when the incantatory and iridescent
are what he's after

not the cuffs of your sweaters
not the corner of any closet
(have you seen how light out
from under the doors makes the cleanest slit?)

silver of their wings
comes off on your hands
so you're not stained with blood, but flight
wander is a film like any other
is a shadow placed along the skin

if he could he might eat light
the way sky takes time to digest firework
the way flesh pants for the vitamin of sun

futures clench like driftwood
and bloom like it when immolated
vigor or ache, either are flammable,
swallowed up in brilliant

it's too mathless, this billow concentrate, opulent quell

that whimper so acute it can't even be backlit
flailing because his wings and speck of heart
don't agree, toward the threshold of metaphor

thirsty because that exoskeleton is too porous,
symbolism's well dries up

one entire illumine has to be enough

Ellen Goldsmith

Shavings

Once I put time in a suitcase with twelve silk scarves.

When I returned to my first house, no hint
of the people who lived there, only a pink kitchen.

In every mirror I look so much better than in any photo.

I just noticed. It's missing from my earring box, a tiny diamond earring,
chipped from my dead grandfather's ring, passed on to me when my father died.

In my house half the rooms don't have doors and all the doors are half open.

Lola Haskins

It

Not-its cross in the air like twilight bats. The slowest counts to ten, her face hidden in her hands. And what when she finishes? Will she part the azaleas one by one, finding only pink wilted trumpets there? Will she crawl under the empty house, where wasps lie hatching in their paper tunnels? Will she cast door-shaped light into the tool shed? Will she stalk the cherry bush as her friend holds her flowered breath? Will she lift a step to find her webby sister? Will she creep around the woodpile to spot her brother, curled behind precarious logs? Or will she go instead to her room under the eaves? Does she know what she has? Does she know she can make them hide forever?

Lola Haskins

The Love Song of Frances Jane
—*after Francis Jammes*

As my hours fold into twisting alleys, I want to choose a sheep to ride, as sheep have pleased me. I take my stick and scour the wide highways. When I find only cement and sooty air, dark as lambs born wrong, I become angry and say oh donkeys, my friends, I am Frances Jane and I am going to heaven.

And I will find moors there, broad as my body when it covers a man. And there will be skies there that are never simply blue, because good and evil will live in them equally. And there will be mosses there, seducing the high hollows, in which I will sink to my thighs and feel I am drowning. And there will be tor-tops there where everything has already been eaten but still the sheep graze and grow fat. And the sheep there will not run from me but allow me to ride them at my will.

I am Frances Jane and I am going to heaven. I will not live any more in this bowl as if I am something floating in soup. I will take only my feet, and my stick because I am half-blind with this life and must tap my way. I will climb to where the stone houses fade then break apart in the wind. I will stand at the top and turn to the four directions, and in each, my robe will stream behind me.

Then I will look up at the one sky, in which every smallest flower of the field, every insect that crawled between petals or lifted up the ground, every small hair that's craved another, every flat hand raised to hurt, has materialized and melted into something else. And I'll spin with wide arms. And when the world blends, *I am Frances Jane*, I will say. *Frances Jane*. And the God-wind that never leaves the tops will blow back into my face everything I am and will be to you, as I cover you with my nakedness and look down into your eyes.

Sara Henning

Disassociation Aubade

Like dusk silking off
the metallic torso
of a banded
demoiselle,
or the riptide

gloss of river
water flecking
and glistening
in dawn's
vanishing

hymnal, or even
like bream coaxing
through spume
and hush,
each dorsal fin

a violent halo,
her father's hands
unbruise her body
before they begin
to disappear.

Andrea Hollander

"Mind Is East Hidden by Trees"

That's what my friend wrote, meaning to type
not *mind* but *mine*, referring to the position
of her house in a photograph. But I read it
as she wrote it—so often that's exactly
the way it is for me, as though my mind
has a mind of its own, and no matter
how I try to cajole it, it seems to slither
snakelike and remain always out of reach,
always *the* mind, not mine.

I think of my father's mind, too, and the way
every time we visited it was as though someone
had removed some of his mind's furniture but only
one piece at a time so we didn't notice at first.
Things just seemed rearranged but not missing,
until one day there might be no place to sit,
we had to stand and hold our bowls in our hands.
The next time we had to hold the food in our hands
and later there would be no food and our hands
would be empty.

But even then my father's mind wouldn't be
empty exactly. Perhaps there'd been a series
of rain storms and afterwards a flood rushed in
that left so much mud behind that even without
the furniture, we couldn't get in, more and more
mud pushing in and staying and with it odd
sea creatures he didn't recognize any more
than he recognized us, his mind east, hidden by
so many trees we couldn't see the forest for them.

Michael Homolka

Rhapsody with Fever

Baldnesses insinuate
among the lapsed tufts
where memory defers
and hills out the window
grow boingy and noncommittal
The trees drop their needles
(some are the trees
and some are my thoughts)
as not this says the breeze
not this and not this either
The family I'm going
to return to one day
flitters somewhere
skin still soft as balloons
Windows more acute
to light than the sky my father
lies months with a fever
bright summer day
after bright summer day
child at the edge of a field
in bed miserable
and none of us helping
none of us really born

Kathryn Hunt

Ursa Major Prowls the Chugach Range

To howl, they said, I came along
and woke the other babies in their
bassinettes. Breath heaved me to
the antiseptic mess, the glare, my
mother's breast. I was daughter two.
The other one already clung to Mama.

O what Arctic dark raged down
to rake away the moon and fill my
mouth with snow. Bears clawed
boreal to North, eyed the runes
as hunters do. Caribou shook
stars from sky, I heard their hooves
engrave the iron ice. Spirit-licked,
daubed red, I heard my mother's cry.
That howl. I joined her.

Rochelle Hurt

Middling

At half past nine the park is a palace
of teenage bombast & angst-gilded crime.
Too proud to be vandals, we hike & heel
half-miles at a time. Into the woods we go,
packing spliffs & a beer & a half-hit
of Cory's blow. He splits it all with me
because I'm *chill*, though I know it's because
I live uptown, straddling the tracks. His hands
are little ghosts flying around his face
as he rants about dads & cops & class.
His lips are little aneurisms in my eye
so when he says my name, I go half-blind.
Corey half-jokes that our joint is laced
with angel dust. Lovely name I say & unswallow
all the air I'll need for a lifetime. We weep
laughter on our backs & our throats are flutes
for calling half-thoughts back to our bodies.
Gold lid-lacquer seeps into my pupils & the clouds
pulse a glinting with my blood's half-beats. I slip
from my sleeves, pull my jeans to my knees.
In this dead time, I make my own sublime.
Come to me with your college dreams, I sing
to my mom. I'm halfway toward happy, finally.
Come to me with scholarships & church
& two-car garages housing shiny husbands.
Come to me with every half-uttered almost
clogging your mouth like a mulch of dead leaves.
Come scatter them now at my half-bare feet.

Rochelle Hurt

The Incorruptible Head of St. Catherine of Siena

*Build a cell inside your mind,
from which you can never flee.*
—St. Catherine of Siena

It was my god-whip, this red need
for something new & new & new. Then you

appeared at my door dressed in that word
like leather: *temporary*. Just a crush,

so I threw myself into our clutch & stutter act,
that bright brain-shatter, wet O-cry. Except—

funny—mine was always an *I, I, I*: the self
pulverized. When we were together,

I was nothing but this stretched vowel, bodiless
& incorruptible by any means but a mouth

closing—which mine eventually did. Now
you want an explanation: consider a saint

who beat God into her body like a bruise.
Ecstasy was watching herself waste,

into plum and yellow. Yet with death—
funny—her wasting ceased. Miraculous,

her sweet-smelling head was severed
& smuggled away by devotees, desperate

to get into her god-cage. At home,
they reached into their sack & pulled out

only fresh roses. Kept supple, see:
my new pain of being not-yours—

self-inflicted but no less exciting.
Forced to be a body wanting, my *I*

is now a pink tendon plucked alone at night.
Understand: you would have tried

to preserve me. So I'm gone. But if you must, go on
& cradle my head, just a skullful of petals.

Safia Jama

Oil Miniature in a Bone Frame

Sunday afternoons
die in a tiny jar.

A cluster of ripe figs, run over
the silver rim. Unholy.

Spit blood, begin again.

A cup and saucer, empty
save a dead louse.

A window, a fallow field. A mouse.

A card table draped in thin velvet.
Small hand prints like a stain.

Sliver of wild moss inside a gun.
Flourishing shadows.

Blue & white China.

This life

a cake that cries out
as you cut.

Willie James

Andrew Wyeth: Helga

1.

I imagine him insisting
to paint her there

Chair pulled so close she watched
an ocean
swirl beneath her
like a soup-filled bowl of barking dogs

his wedges scrape
        attempting for a coarser beauty

like mackerel
or brining pickle jars
        shucked mollusks
melting on a heel of palm

He kept these private for almost 15 years
hiding her image inside chests
of winter coats
            peeking only inward
to see her tiptoe across a pocket

He's hewing
        a stone he will not skip
        and her gaze
slightly askew
strews like sieve through water

Willie James

2.

                    In winter Boston
I was those dogs
and I too was Helga
watching them
their lips uncurl to
well bred teeth

You'll be poor for years Will
George said   We boiled
water   spoke
of mid-terms   Joseph Stalin's
20th Century

*You gotta love the Russians
Will*   He was talking
militarily   A boy's mind
canonizing a Cossack's force   while
a fresh snow seizes

statues of minutemen
lining Lexington green   burials
of white bodies under snow   *We'll
all kick the bucket one day* Will
This I know   This I know

3.

Helga
this isn't much
this bowl
of hair
I want you to have it

I've taken the coat off my body
and pink as a cat's tongue I enter the world

Take my mammal
I leave its cruel
kingdom to the fleas   except

I'll miss your hair
the ripe peach of
each armpit   and ear pressed

no larger than a fetus
to belly   Something like a whale sings

in herds in baths
on farms of ocean   Which is to say

Take this bowl   I want to leave

Brionne Janae

Naked Pizza Friday

like buoys bobbing in the harbor,
the limp cocks dangled between over pasty thighs
and the breasts of the women swayed too, droll sea of nakedness
lolling and cloaked in evergreens and drooping tree branches, lit
with a loosely hanging rainbow of party lamps—
how did you get here— schlepping up Berkeley hills,
your friend clucking at the *sluttiness* of girls flocking
like *fucking geese in hoe shoes*— then stepping
onto the patio past the veil into eden
and the sudden pink of nipples hard and staring.
you had only heard *free* and *pizza* and *friday* and are wholly
unprepared for this transition into pre-fallen grace.
virginal in your long white skirt you fidgeted
with the few clothed folk on the periphery. not for years after
would you chuckle and wish you had gone naked too.
not till that frigid city where you learned to dance
and throw your hips around recklessly and with purpose,
to arch your back lift your breast and twirl
not till you learned we are bodies first,
animals moving from ecstasy to ecstasy
and the only way to the spirit is flesh.

Lesley Jenike

Black Heart

Lead Belly's grey goose is vengeance incarnate
because the damn thing won't die, won't be slapped
back to human periphery

when he's got his eye trained on the whole sky,
be damned. Weird hero for a children's song,
that zombie goose, leathery to the point

of breaking the knife's blade and the saw's tooth
some fool used to try and cut him, couldn't
be cooked and made tender by the fire,

couldn't be plucked by *my wife or your wife*
for the soft pillow, couldn't be made straight
by the shaft of a shotgun. Blam! We watch,

by song's end, our living dead fly north
with a long string of goslings, Lord, Lord, Lord:
a wild humor finds its own gag reel,

I guess. Blame the bland Burl Ives version
for the white seep, but while my newborn sleeps
the breast pump sings (*black heart, black heart, black*

heart), and I render time down to a balm
for easing the hurt. That grey goose, in-
between-day-and-night goose, might grow sick, some-

times, of never, not ever giving in,
and when he sleeps in the blue it's not rest,
with its storms, soot, and hawks, no more safe

Lesley Jenike

than would be the knife, the gun, the fire.
What doesn't kill us makes us bitter, goes
the canard, but makes the honking sweet

knowing we persist for our offspring, no
matter how ugly the wing: this line
kinked on my gut, breasts sucked in by the pump

(*black heart, black heart, black heart*) and the white milk
mined by the ache-full, bright against
the dark bottle. Now come the midnight train.

Joe Jiménez

A pencil and a bowlful of pears.

Often, I wish I'd been with more men.
Sadly, but sadly, a man's body
is the slingshot I feared.
Simple impossible tenderness.
Dreamscapes and butterscotch, Listerine
and landmines.
I can't tell you one kind of madman
from a handful of teeth.
I can't tell sadness from a pencil
and a bowlful of pears.

But I can tell you my body is a nest braided
from hush,
a catapult of upthrown stones.

Breath is more bitter when it empties
its hands
into cuffs,

and the world may have built us from ribs,
or from mud.
I don't care. I don't.

In the rucksack of hog belly and gloves, I
still
ask God,
Why am I not quelled enough by shadows
that sweat? How might I undo
this slack? Or widen my throatbone
so I swallow shit best?

The answer
is a shadow that kisses its own fists, a tooth
willing to eat any darkness;

Joe Jiménez

the answer
is who hasn't ever wanted to unbitter
his body?

All night I might fathom taking back
something precious

that somehow,
long ago, or not so long, I don't know,
ripped off,
yanked from bone,
sloughed off like a husk.

The truth about loneliness is it's lonely.

The truth about lonely is it lasts.

For whole moments, lifespans,
less so.

But to clutch and to glow, to hatch,
to show…

Isn't that the point of the point we are
making with breath?

Once in a coffee shop,
I watched
a man sketch a handful of pears.

So it might last, I wanted to place
my parts
in his bowl—
palms or mouth or asshole.
O, does it matter?
None of it sits well when I say it
out loud.

These words as strangers I can't make
myself finish off and eat.

Erin Jones

Dream Him Dead

In the field, the cattle flop against the earth,
become puddles.
We are hushed under these hot spells too.

Eventually we'll stop listening like our mothers did.
I think of you
nodding your head when he tells you to change,

his mouth at your ear, personal humidity.
In a book you lent me,
you left a list you wrote for yourself: *Pretend you are water;*

Dream him dead. Like all the girls
herded to this town,
you are shown to the field. When you watch

the mechanism, the gate unlatching
like a quick mouth,
you almost convince yourself to run.

Jason Joyce

Succulents

I saw the future with her clothes off

A Happy Meal-ness, sinking ship tingling
climbing the rope in gym class

In order we go: her, me, the door

She sleeps in my tank top, XL

Sheets of past ghosts tumble the laundry sea,
when right words didn't come out,
no longer haunting the house, my mouth

A hickory sadness she cannot teach,
walking downtown in winter, layers I must keep. I am
a desperate child unwrapping an entire
Christmas of underwear and socks, things I need.

Her touch says we wander
eternal, bags in hand, under eyes, rings
and reclaimed wood, the same bed

I cannot wait to not go home without her

A future of creatures, XS

Strands of desert vines entwined, repotting the
succulents, thirsty all these years,
soothsayers praying:

Let there be ocean where we finally unravel

Kendra Langdon Juskus

How to Die in Peru

Peel your fear like a fruit,
and the lemon-eyed monkeys will come.
One will trade its terror with you,
sinking the teeth of it
in your wrist. From that point,
                      think only of dying.

Take a river boat from Yurimaguas to Iquitos.
Follow the rasped rumor of pink dolphins
on muddy waters.
Pour each outrageous sunset
over your hands your arms
the hair of the one you love
like grenadine.

Do not let your death
        out of your sight.

In lifting the whiskers of a coconut
to your lips or licking mango juice
from the inside of your elbow,
do not lose your grip on your death.
Do not lose your taste for it,
when the *siete raices* in the brown bottle
drags its nails down your throat
each night on the boat
where everyone cocoons in their hammocks
and no one else thinks of your death.
                      You must not forget it.

Kendra Langdon Juskus

Do not lend it, in the neon night
of Iquitos, to the American businessmen
or the Indian girls on their arms,
the artists hawking their heartswork on the river flats:
do not give it away,
           they have their own deaths to die.

Hold it, hold it
in your mouth like a day-glow
Peru Libre, like the toast given before the *Libre*,
to the future.

Leah Claire Kaminski

After Reading James Wright

My body thrums, works itself slightly up
off this someone else's bed, layered
up from the air it's in is where my body
is as I'm thinking about being here—
I mean, looking out the window here,
with the strawberries and pomegranates, redwood and gingko
variously wilting and plumping and thrusting
outside and it's very hot, and it's someone else's
home and very particular in that but sentences are
everywhere or they are inside me   [*Over my head, I see* object
                                                                          object modifier
                                                                          object modifier.
                                                                          Prepositional phrase
                                                                          The cowbells follow one another
                                                                          indirect object.
                                                                          Prepositional phrase
                                                                          prepositional phrase
                                                                          The droppings of last year's horses
                                                                          verb phrase.
                                                                          SVO, subject modifier.
                                                                          SVO, *looking for home.*
                                                                          SVO.]
and so sentences don't help and my body is very tired, thrumming tired
from nothing much but being in my head so what is it to be here, or is it nothing
when the crack in the root of my front tooth
is my place, my tongue loves to probe it for pain and it is my deepest home
nor can I peel off the palimpsest
of elsewheres when everywhere
looks somewhat like everywhere else / has a point
of comparison / pinpoint pivot to turn this place
into that,   North Star in a hydrangea panicle
                North Wind in what the air picks up from an otter's sleek head

Leah Claire Kaminski

    and how to be in
a place & its own muscles moving mine
or is it I should try to feel the same everywhere, I don't
really understand the goal of mindfulness
but they say it reduces pain, and   yes if it could slow time down too
so my dad isn't 4 inches shorter than he was 5 years
ago, and my womb more juicy, or if it could have taken
longer, placing feet over time stretched not pinched
then sign me up; there's a Buddha in the backyard; he is backlit to effect and I have
tired myself out, many times over, staring at the ceiling of another childhood's bedroom:
when there are the dead and the killed and my blood is vesseled here, and here and here

Kara Krewer

Human Eyes

Look closely at the pear's flesh
and the sunken mark of your thumb,
      an unnerving acceptance.

Star-shaped cells
that make the fruit crunch:
      sclereids, from *skleros*, meaning hard.

So many ancient Greek philosophers
telling ancient dick jokes—
      Skleros! Ha!

Also, sclera, pupil's white tunic.
Touch my eye. It is actually
      quite tough,

though it is the part the ants
eat first, the sweetest, easiest
      way in.

Peter Krumbach

The Duck

It was the moment when all eight of us
suffered the same seizure, the one
that marks each dinner party,
the instant of sticky silence
when you pretend to eat the duck,
trawling your halted mind for a thing
to say. It was then that I startled myself
proposing that we all undress.
I suspected you would be the first to get
on board, maybe your sister Lydia, and Stan,
her husband, who had spent the evening
eyeing Yolanda, whose one reckless breath
could have burst her tube top into confetti.
Perhaps the blue-cheeked man brooding
to my left like an unfinished statue
of Richard Nixon.
But no - it was old Professor Lustig
who stood up at the head of the table,
and in the gleam of his wife's cutlery
began to loosen his tie.

Arden Levine

Cake

I.
It used to be just for special occasions, like birthday parties
or as a reward for behaving on a car trip. Now
I can eat it all the time, just like I told myself I would
when I grew up, even if there's nothing special at all.

When I got married, I ate leftover cake out of Tupperware
for weeks. The wedding cake had vanilla frosting,
and each layer something different in between:
raspberry jam, chocolate ganache, orange marmalade.
There were also rehearsal dinner cakes, and those
were almond with hazelnut cream. It pleased me
to sit on the new couch with the Tupperware
and slide cake between my lips, mouthful after mouthful
into my young, lovely body. For a little while
after I divorced, I bought individual cake slices for dinner
and ate them with my fingers. *Why not?* I asked the empty living room.

II.
It's not that I have any particular fondness for cake.
It's that it is usually delightful and desirable and a bit forbidden
in a way that women wish to be much of the time.

III.
That pastry chef girl in the subway ads is
a hipster Betty Crocker. Her whole look is a triumph,
especially the horizontal-striped shirt, which reveals
a substantial bustline, clearly delectable as her baked treats.
Anyone would want to give her a big hug, or kiss that mouth,
which perhaps has a buttercream flavor. But I'd bet

Arden Levine

she doesn't actually devour those adorable cupcakes
(or she eats just one, like a good girl. Or takes just a bite
for the camera, even more sensible).

IV.
Some websites are devoted entirely to cakes, with pictures
and recipes and captions about who made them and why:
children's cakes piped with boisterous cartoon text,
teacakes upon glass displays upon white wicker furniture upon
Technicolor grass, exquisite petit fours with gumpaste daisies
so real I expect that unwelcome insects try to pollinate them,
sheet cakes with fondant like ironed tablecloths.

But I get very sad somehow, knowing that these cakes will be eaten,
or worse, thrown away (or worse, that these aren't even real cakes).

On one site was a story about a lady who threw a picnic party
and had made a meatloaf that looked like a carrot cake
(with mashed potato icing!) paired with small cakes
that looked like grilled cheese sandwiches.
Her guests were confused and delighted, because how witty
to create a prank that is also a meal and everyone has fun in the end.

V.
Usually after dinner, I go running. I can't run as far
as I did when I was younger, but I get some good thinking done,
or I daydream while I watch the scenery
fall slowly behind me. I have one daydream in which a man
with a very pleasant face presents me with a bouquet of roses,
and I have to look hard to see that the petals
are made of the most precisely sliced sections of cake.
Together, we peel them, one by one, away
from the stem and the stamen and feed them to each other.

Jeffrey Little

Lost King Forward

I am tied to an office chair in a roomful of naked children,
each one painted a dissimilar shade of blue with a bird's
nest knotted into his or her hair. This is Europe, as seen
from the side. Lost King Forward slowly rises from a pile

of oak leaves and takes a single step away from the fire,
he has a pocket watch and a basket of reeds. A factory
here eats starlight and shits fine blocks of steel. Outside,
the forked catechisms of the old dialogues endure. She

told me she'd decided to name the groundhog Waldorf
as if this explained everything away, and now, like two
lurching fiefdoms with a nebulous past, finally we could
both move on. The forest however is filled with crumbs.

One good look at the sky will tell you, legs aren't worth
much anymore. Go ahead, ask all those stars in the tips
of the weeds wet with rain, they'll tell you, the difference
between a kneecap and an army that's danced for its food.

Ginna Luck

The Problem With Grief Is That It Never Lets Me...

Under my dress or inside of a mountain, between the bold color of my heart and a lonely piece of trash everything is blunt and dangerous. I am failing to see what is right in front of me. Instead of a moon halved by the fog I see a bridge blowing apart into heaps and twists of wood. Instead of an iced over lake I see miles of mountain road split between swamp and a burning swirl of grass. Instead of a constellation of stars I see a man who is difficult to love. It is just black woods out here adding night after overgrown night into thinking I've never (not) loved him. To hold him seems as unlikely as holding an echo firmly under my tongue. The sky, from this distance, looks synthetic and mud colored, makes my arms, my whole body ache, not for seeing clearly but from calling and calling into wind and frozen. I remain a language hardened by wind chill. My lips spit lonely out as a metaphor for an actual opening. And no, lonely does not open, not in a place like this, waiting for the same hands to float back, listening for the hard line of the horizon to answer with an entrance. Instead of the snow there is falling shadow. Instead of sinking into sleep there is the fog of not knowing. How far can a mind wander before it is dream drunk and coughing up dead ends? Love is an icicle hanging in the sky I have chosen to trust. It will glow inside and be iridescent and I will try to hold it tight against me.

Cody Lumpkin

Heavy Winter Coat

It hangs on a rack, a depressed roommate
who watches everything and judges me.

After a couple of winters, it's so out of style.
All those zippered pockets I could never fill.

With money spent on other things, I dress
myself in this suitable warmth. My hands

discover lost gloves, a five dollar bill, receipts
to things I thought would make me happy.

DM Macormic

Now That His Husband Is Gone, He Wears Only Dresses

In a city park so busy
    it almost seems private,

my father cuts across
    damp fields. His gown drags

a showy train of crimson
    silk, wetted dark & dull.

Near a pond, he pulls apart
    bits of stale bread for fish.

Sowing crumbs from his fist,
    he watches the surface breach

like glass above the place
    where mouths hurry open.

He's too tall not to hasten
    families as they pass him

whatever he is; part boy, part
    hair panicked & blonde, legs

of unanswered prayer. And who is
    to blame for this crude delivery

of a body when there isn't
    a midwife for this kind of birth?

He sends his loss in a card. Inside,
    a picture I drew for him when

I was a child. Between a green ribbon
    for earth, & a sky unmistakably blue

two scribbly men are holding hands,
    their giant fingers knotted together.

Lauren Mallett

Requiem for an Unseeable Gravity

The trouble is words.
I don't say *what we've built around us is breaking*.
I don't tell him *the birds aren't migrating like they used to*.
Instead I worry about the roads, progress, E. coli, and its helix tail.
In a novel a woman lists what she has loved about the earth:
fear of heights, Nebraska sky, coffee, wind. I believe her,
and I believe Duane rode into the sea on the back of his horse.
Loved the earth but could not stay.
Like Dalva I prefer *undiminished consciousness,*
but sometimes being awake is so goddamn exhausting.
So I installed a sunset on my computer.
The blue lights living there slowly *f.lux*. Is what
the program is called. That is, the screen palette yellows
in steps. Second-long shifts meant to mimic sundown. *There
it goes* so that supposedly my light receptors can calm.
I tell him this, while perched on a picnic table
on the bar's back patio lit up for mood. The Buddha sits
next to a truck tire. The only ceiling is a ladder,
its one end fastened to the roof's edge and the other
to the plywood fence. I curl my hands around the bars
just to feel *how loose*. How the unfinished rung
shifts in its dowel holes whichever way I pull.

Cynthia Manick

Southern Impression

       Once in a cup
of pressed   strawberries
covered in cold
       well-water, I saw
minor galaxies
       and hieroglyphics.
One contained
       pomade
       from my grandfather's
shop-
           the smell
      of tipped hats
and a greasy ring
        strong
enough
to jump-
start
    your left
    ventricle.
His wife   my grandmother
    yelling
     about God-
how he made
    streets
with no stop
    lights
        just the cross ings
of brown
    bodies,
    crocodiles
       and trash
before burning.

Gail Martin

Just When We Are Lost

The neurologist wants me to believe dreams are mechanical, tired neurons trying to reattach, reorganize, following connections dropped like bread crumbs in the forest. Waking, there's often the sound of paper tearing, the plink plink of peanuts filling up the gas line. And just when we are lost and forget which side of the body our heart is on, we are given the dream of a girl drinking her milk, eating deep cake where the center piece is entirely frosting. Or glide through a clearing where April stands drying herself beside the river, pulling on her long green gloves.

Brooke McKinney

Killing the Leaves

I don't guess I'll ever get over that child saving me from becoming a pile of meat and blood. The streets covered in urine and blood, anyway.

You'd think these roads were nothing but remains of humans once in love. I wrote notes on the back of cigarettes and coined a new term for help—*please*.

The trees were dying quicker than we were, spraying for mosquitoes, killing the leaves becoming lungs becoming leaves becoming stiff.

Now that I'm back home, I want to shoot my daddy, though his name isn't *Charlie*. I thank mama for having a stroke—saving me from the filth of the frontline.

Driving home sometimes, the sunset stands down behind the trees, bursting into a thousand fires between those veins of branches, killing the leaves in the rearview mirror…

I hit the brakes. I yell, Ceasefire! Goddamn that sticker—*Objects in mirror are closer than they appear.*

Rachel Mennies

Removing Him from the Sex Scenes in All of Your Books

You don't touch him. You never touch him.
Your hands reopen the book and crease the pages.
You worship each new man the protagonist fucks
and leaves. You are ready for all the freshman boys

in Hollis Hall. You march down Brattle Street
from the library, fed. He sells used Hondas
a few left turns from your childhood
home. You close the book again. He becomes

a doctor, performs the world's first-ever
head-to-head transplant. He has children, then
never has children. You turn to a new chapter.
He joins the Air Force. He opens

a bakery. His hands knead the growing
soft white. Is he hot from the work, reaching
to open the window? Is it loud on the dawn
Boston street? You don't write

about him. You return one stack of books
and withdraw another. You whisper
Your gardens were the gardens I spoke of
when I spoke to you of gardens to strangers

on the T. Would he cover your eyes, too,
with his fingers? Would he *take you* in the museum
hallway, in the backseat of Cairo taxicabs?
You don't touch him. You never touch him.

You count the doors again on the all-boys' floor.
You open one, pushing a blank young face
to yours. Remember how
he never loved you. Remember

to write that down.

Faisal Mohyuddin

Partition, and Then

We were looking for _____ we found _____.
—Carolyn Forché

The night is an empty basket, and the long journey ahead
promises to be weighed down by hunger, luminous

and wild. As they cross into the newly formed nation,
a child, cargo strapped to her mother's back, takes the black

sheet of the sky, folds it seven times to make a horse,
then fashions wings for it knitted from thin ribbons of wind.

Inside the brick temple of her mother's grasping heart,
a burning nest of nightjars, their feathers flecked with both

copper's shimmer and its blue decay. Their calls are like stones
skipping across the surface of a river. Before the new day

tears open the stillness of her reveries, the girl rests her cheek
between her mother's shoulders and rolls herself back into

the womb. Inside, the rivers of the newly broken world
flow backwards toward the Himalayas, returning first to snow,

then to cloud. At the first blue blush of dawn, the child
begins to collect the stars, loses count, begins again, and then

again, until sleep arrives and she becomes a white ember of light,
exiled from her sky. In the distance, blindfolded theologians

straddle the gash drawn by Mountbatten's pen, holding vials
of new blood, large spoons carved from ivory, and honey.

Carolyn Moore

Dear John Letter

Hey, it's me—the grit in your oyster that never turned
to pearl—writing to you, cigarette butt in my salad
before I finished lunch. Whatthehell were you doing
in last night's storm, knocking at my dream door
after all these years of leaving me alone,
in peace? Was it because your new wife phoned, edgy,
quavering, duty-bound to share your news?
I slipped into my better-you-than-I apron
and served her alas sandwiches of *ooh* and *ah*,
with a side of pardon, free of charge. My dream door,
back to that—what was your point in tracking mud
to its welcome mat with nothing new to *tsk* or *blub*?
And why did we pretend that you still lived?

Jennifer Moss

A Spider Climbs A Thread and Sets its Web Aquiver

Watch where the long line comes out of a life:
we are looped in it, living in it like the weather
lives in it, like the spider moves the fly
from pain into oblivion.
We who lose our way think
we have lost our home.
But no: home slowly, tightly, wraps itself around us.

Benjamin Nash

The Wig

Dignified, stately,
I was going to argue
that separation of
powers also meant
division of labor,
specialization, but
it fell off, a horse
stepped on it, a man
spit tobacco on it,
it turned brown, a
cat was seen playing
with it and I decided
not to go, smell it
all day, deal with
the blue jay, Madison
and his jokes, or have
Franklin, the others
stare at it, whisper,
faction against me.

Erik Norbie

Marine Life Thrives in Unlikely Place: Offshore Oil Rigs
—*New York Times* headline

Fish will school the skulls
of our homes too

someday when the arctic icecap drowns.
And homestead the first floors

of our high-rises
after the algae have pioneered in.

It's not surprising
given our femurs

were once steel girders
that our first cells barnacled to.

Even now, the studies say,
we are as much bacteria

as human—an ocean of species
plumbing the hulls of our abdomens.

Because every life becomes
a scaffold for another one:

the swinging crane of sunlight
assembling new canopies,

the grow box of a coffin
blossoming with annelids,

the parting gift of a footprint held
open like a hand.

Olivia Olson

The Teacher in Town

walked late into the night, collecting images. When he got home, he would lay the images out on his desk like stones and sort them. Every night he did this, and every night, he felt as if the man who searched for images was different than the man who sorted them like stones. The man hunched over sorting resented the man who walked freely, and the walking man resented the greed of the man waiting at home, hungry for stones. Both men grew hatred inside of them. The walking man began to bring home stranger and stranger images, challenging the man at home to find a useful way to sort them. The man at home set them in great ugly forms that the walking man felt were a waste of time. One night, the walking man blinded himself to all the images he saw and brought nothing to the man at home. They spoke little after that, and just let the fire in the hearth light his face in unexpected bursts until it was time to sleep.

Pablo Otavalo

Outside Utica

The bruise of sky behind shoulder-high cornstalks,
perpetual halogen sunset, the last trace of city lights
beyond the horizon. We came for the heron, the Perseid
meteor shower, the lightning bugs. One kiss from eloping,
letting cicadas officiate vows to the Milky Way Almighty, carried
away on the sweet reek of topsoil, milkweed, and sumac. Ours
the clover field behind the Cattail Inn, ours the empty road
from here to Ottawa, ours the nightjar calls
from the woodland's edge, and ours the Little Dipper
claiming the northern sky.
                                        In the morning,
outside a pizza parlor that served coffee till eleven, we sat
on a pinewood bench, squinting into the sun, before us
a wall of corn, beside us vacant storefronts, and a cloud of dust
and gravel chasing a truck like a mutt.

Eric Pankey

The Hyenas

A pair of hyenas stood at the door, dressed not unlike missionaries: black pants, white button down shirts, their backpacks a little too snug under their armpits.

One said—*We agree with John Cage, art should not be used as self-expression but as self-alteration.*

The other said—*Or consider what Rene Char said about why he became a writer: A bird's feather on my windowpane in winter and all at once there arose in my heart a battle of embers never to subside again.*

Before I could get a word in edgewise, the one said—quoting, I think, Gaston Bachelard—*If a poet looks through a microscope or a telescope, he always sees the same thing.*

I had to admit these were some smart hyenas. Yet each time they spoke, their hackles went up and whatever they said felt like a threat. Not to mention the snickering, the tee-hee-ing, the saliva matting their chin hairs.

I stood in the doorframe. I had forgotten whether hyenas are scavengers or predators. I didn't want them entering.

I really have to go—I said, but the one hyena put his paw between the screen and the jamb.

Okay—he said—*but before we go, remember what Horace said*—*Many brave men lived before Agamemnon, but all are overwhelmed in eternal night, unwept, unknown, because they lack a sacred poet.*

The other hyena, tugging his friend away by a backpack strap, attempting to ease the tension, said to me—*Perhaps you are just that sacred poet.*

Casey Patrick

AIR TEMPERATURE 82
AIR TEMPERATURE 82
CALM CALM SWELL

Repeat & repeat. Each morning the weather report given up to radio waves & somewhere a receiver. The farther you get the more it's *accurate forecast difficult* like shouldn't you know better. Each day less sure, more sky turned whale belly, so blue I spend hours open-mouthed. It's why I make a perfect messenger. *Conditions appear generally average*: pure guesswork. Average means nothing in a place no one's been, which is nearly all of it. Same shape: compass & cross, & at times I bless you in the names of North South East West, rosary repetition to pass time on this slim shingle of sand. I forget myself; you don't pray. *Direction east swell direction east*, amen. Something like that maybe. Waiting each night for your next signal. Forgive me for forgetting the ocean is wide. But you're so close to heaven now & we'd like to know what it is you see.

Milorad Pejić
translated from the Bosnian by Omer Hadžiselimović

Picking Up Baggage

We are the same as our suitcases. At the baggage
carousel, it seems as though we, a little anxious,
are waiting for our very selves. All eyes are fixed
at the rubber curtain of the tunnel that should begin
coughing out our things. When the conveyor belt
starts moving, looking as if I.D. cards were sliding
on it, I can guess which hand will take which bag.
Mine is not coming out yet.

Our lives are assigned the fates of our suitcases.
The great love story begins with a scuffle in which
the leather tongue on the bag of a young au-pair
from Izmir latches onto the aluminum suitcase
of a bearded rocker from San Francisco. A long
(and tragic) journey through the desert awaits
the German trekker who, impatient, pushes through
to a backpack the size of a dead cow. The sleeve
of a silk shirt is dragging behind a ripped Ikea bag
like a gut. No sight of mine yet.

As if wedded to our loads, at the carousel we stare
at only one point. My bag is an unhappily married
woman who is in no hurry to get to the exit.

Seth Pennington

I Drive You Through Mosquito Truck Spray

Looking for where we can't be
seen, cruising through the one stop light,

our shirts stick to the damp caught
between our shoulders and the seat back.

I drive you through mosquito truck spray,
that dust that blows out the southern sun.

I roll up the windows and turn off the air,
say, don't breathe, don't breathe that in.

Next to the soy field-cum-golf course,
I park in the poor part of the city

cemetery, where if luck holds you, maybe
you might have a white stone, but your name's

a gone thing, washed so each stone is soap clean.
In high school it was brave to drink with the dead.

Kissing over them was a sure
curse, one no one had ever heard said.

Across the highway, MFA Oil is a bleached desert,
save the moths ecstatic and strobing in the far light. You keep

staring into their nervous pulse.
I am making promises into your neck and lay

back your seat to a deep song, the engine
off but panting, steaming the sudden dewfall

so it rises through the magnolia air
and makes clouds that tomorrow we'll drink like moon-

shine and remember what power
we have to take a place, the boneyards of our youths,

to wreck all those deaths until what we taste
in the hot night is not sour, but our own thrill.

Lizzy Petersen

Duration

Durée de vie printed on the box of
lightbulbs stacked in the employee bathroom.
Something something life, that is
a measurement. Endurance,

hurdle of light. Time, let me shape you
into a span: The hour the butterfly's
wings inflate—a reach, a finger
stretched back on the hand—

and the trigger between memory
and memory. Fluorescent. Taking
precious time to turn on but goes out like a—
a light, I guess. A dead phone

fills space, an autumnal tulip. Crowds.
Persists. I lose its charger and
sure enough I grow less and less
certain of midnight's low blue glow.

Robbie Pock

Letter to a Danish Skeleton
*—The Vedbaek Woman and Child,
National Museum Copenhagen
Late Mesolithic 5000 BC*

You are mostly intact here in the future
though there is a dent in your skull and
your pelvis is spread like a big ocean fish
split down the middle.

Also, your ribcage has collapsed
and your unhinged clavicles have drifted a little
with the sediment.

I don't know what to say about the boy
except he's with you. His gaping
mouth, like tallow or wax, melted
over your arm through the long time.

So little is left of the rest of him–
splintered bones like twigs or reeds
gone brittle in winter. Amulets
have collected in the cavity where his belly was.

I can tell you that the skunks and foxes
won't find him, that you will be together
always in this box of heavy glass.
But there will be light and voices every day.
You will be uncovered forever,
and we all will look
into the spaces between your bones.

Alison Prine

song of a small city

a small city is not an apple

it is not a cathedral or a gown

a small city produces a confetti rain of tree blossoms

in the breath of a small city there are translations and the clinking of coins

here light falls across our faces

here one hour is transplanted into the next

a small city does not recognize its own hands

a small city holds up less sky and is therefore less grand and less weary

a small city does not muscle toward the sea

the distance from the top to the bottom of a small city is one lost shoe

Alison Prine

Other People's Sadness

I don't believe in psychological science
though I see a need for counting:

1) The flattening out and closing in of the sky.
2) How people need to be seen, yet are so unseeing.
3) A sparrow singing inside the airport terminal.
4) The dial which, you discover too late, turns only one way.

Do you see anything the color that matches
what you are trying to rid yourself of?

Chartreuse shining in a glass?
Would it help if we all took a sip?

Is there a sound –
tires turning slowly in the dirt,
the bronchial cough of a stranger?

5) That open water feeling.

Doug Ramspeck

Revival

I am listening this morning to the industry
of bullfrogs, the sermon of crows,

while gazing out the upstairs window
at the prison a half mile down the road,

the hours inside those walls, my father
used to say, not sanded down along

the edges. I remember, when he was dying,
how he told me that the only music

he'd ever truly loved was the drumbeat
of the big guns of the destroyers

in the War. Last night I dreamed
of bullbats rising into a dark sky,

of the bile of clouds above the hickories.
Here was the loneliness of grass

that would dull yellow come winter
in a corrosive wind. And as for the prisoners,

I see them milling by the fence, imagine
that the sounds of their voices are dust

swirling in a field. At night, I suspect,
they lie awake and listen to their breaths,

or dream of sunlight drifting fluted
into water, or imagine that they exist

inside the radiance of memory,
in the nerve endings of stars after dark.

Rebekah Remington

Silverberry

Frumpish flowers take the yard.
Stiff noon puts on its indifferent glare
disturbed only by a medivac dwindling toward the city.

Deep in my life, I watch the earthworm have it out with the robin.
Ordinary battles repeat and repeat:
Remorse and hunger, rhododendron and chokeweed.
Body and the idea of the body.

I know only one language and God is farther than Pluto,
                                      title half revoked,
                                                  spinning out there in the time-space,
caught, they say, in a debris cloud, hoodwinking one of its moons.

It's a human mind I've been given.
When I look up what I see
is blue and a memory of blue,
       white wolf and my father,
          born again among pronghorn and sprung green.
I want to reconcile gratitude and fury, popsongs and death.
I want to trust, once and for all, in the wilderness waiting for me.
Scent of the silverberry. River prattling on.
Breezeless Tuesday, September closing in.

Kylan Rice

Georgic, Tri-Cities

*using what was once military aviation technology
to grow better grapes using pictures from the air*
    Chris Anderson, 'Agricultural Drones'

meaning   don't work so hard
    Pound, Canto 76

i

from an aerial angle would form   rings of green this side the Columbia
    lush to the point the irrigation arms in reaching have   to pivot or
fall back the near   miss of each reach turning to circumference
    to boundary   still bringing in a bounty a bringing forth

from such height a true crop   circle sign of no intruder instead
    intrusion's inverse familiar green   leaves the flesh beneath the leaves
no evidence but readiness   ready for a coming for a breach
    the trespass of a gatherer   a bringing in

o   form
    ring   your double work   in reaching retreat inreaching
coming unbidden   counterpoint to no song I'd thought to sing but was

    singing still stilled   in place hoverer
turner over earth earth-   bound drone unthinking
    worker o o   heat-seeker

ii

openness's   images can be stitched together rendered to a hard-
       drive in the same span   it takes for sound from an out-
cry to cross the crop   from the fixed wing height of an unmanned
       aerial system you can tell   the field its health from light from leaves

reflected then picked   up in the sensor you can tell the protein
       content derive   from it a point cloud o
sensor repaired to a distance on wings   fixed o
       drone o droned the work is done   for me remotely

focus me register   the flourishing gaps of green I've laid among
       high desert folds ensheaver not of deeds' fruition nor their readiness
but readiness's imaging imagine   potential uses now the image is

       stitched by lens less a cherry stone   than a cherry stone-shaped
o   the shock of wheat's creep across the valley shocks into an openness
       gathered   graphed that   wondered over grapheme

iii

and note   the optimized register
       the note the fixed-wing-singing   song's fixity its singers devouring
winged things the swallow the kill   -deer picker at the flesh beneath the leaves

Kylan Rice

     and let the mind not forget its work its sake its deed   ensheaving
doings how a thing is   used to do carry your oar hero

     -figure sign you suffer until it's seen   to be a thresh let it be
free it to be seen a flail enabler of a field   the work it does in reality
    swallowed optimized by wherever's parameter

domain governing seeing that governs anything's disclosing   unclose it
    you've naught   but phenomena harrower tender harrowed
tenderer voyager giver of givens   up remote labor

    survey   at a certain distance the eye growing more open
at a certain distance the shocked cry   the killdeer singing not here not here
    what you're looking for is me o see   my wing its flailing come upon me

José Antonio Rodríguez

Plutonian Nights
—after Bob Hicok

Plutonian nights
Light a thousand margaritas.
A thousand fools exchange
The yes, begin to glass the rain.
Gunfire-close, they raze
A rainforest saying
Something impossible.
Bulbs spring, blushing the sky.
They'd like to touch
The river's decibels, something
Like sipping the life of a poem.

Kathleen Rooney

L'invention Collective

Today isn't what you'd call a beach day, exactly, but then again that isn't exactly a mermaid. Belgium has a coast, Loulou the Pomeranian knows, because he has been there with Georgette and the master, but almost no one thinks of it in association with sexiness. This creature is a creation for that northerly shoreline: a siren in reverse, cold-not-alluring, its seductiveness mucked up by the fact that the fish is stuck, stranded on the sand. Everybody's got to have some prurient interests. Everybody's got to have a little bad taste: blue eye shadow and fur coats, fishscales and skin. The head and fins and torso of a fish – if fish have torsos? – merged with a woman's hips and crotch and legs. It's a mockery, yes, but what's it mocking? The collective invention, Loulou believes. The gills that don't breathe; it's being killed by the air, the fish-eye going dead. But the genitals are there. Loulou heard a misogynist visitor to Magritte's studio say that the being was "a practical man's mermaid" because it is fuckable. If that's the kind of human you are, Loulou thinks, then maybe. The master called the painting "the answer to the problem of the sea." Loulou sees it as an inquiry into the problem of humanity. The sea is itself a solution, if only of saline. Neither the master nor Loulou believes in the insolubility of anything.

Kristen Rouisse

Another Photograph of Appalachia

Fix her babe
against a chest

split with sun;
teenaged and milkless

and sewn with
bone. A mother,

unaware. Small
fistful of paint

petals. Mouth,
unhinged. How

irises ember despite
monochrome.

Despite the hog,
hung and spilling

black thread.
From the mountains,

still-born blue rises.
And the treetops

are weighted with
low-hanging gospel;

the subtlest pinprick
of yesterday's moon.

Leigh Camacho Rourks

For the Wife of Alexander Wood

A parenthetical reference, a scientist's cautionary tale: *the first person to have died from an intravenous overdose was his wife.*

I imagine wind that morning
in Edinburgh / rain / air thick,
smoky from chimneys;

I don't know the date / her age / even
her first name / what he called her, when he called,

only his needle, with its pistons / joints / screws,
its delivery of morphine hydrochloride,
elegant piercing, maybe a shaft of light
caught through a slit in the curtains, its

glint / curves / angles as it pricked
her flesh, again / again / again,

only her pride in her husband,
his fame (his name / their name known
in England / America / the world),
only her willingness

to twist the pieces / to make the machine / to take
his morphine / to stop the shaking / to feel the warm
climb her arm, her face, her brain / to force a wanting
body still / to grow this need / to need
all, all, all the time.

She is recorded
in the bruised.

Recorded in the pocked
and purpled arms
// her arms //
of the women still dying.

caught / snagged / snared / sewed
into the fabric of her story with his needle.
Women / Women / Women / Numbers
at first prescribed then just described
weaker, needing things / soft, needing things
accumulating since her death, who
etched / kept / remembered / buried

her in their soft, broken veins.

Diane Schenker

Heimisch

Home. Hamlet. Haunt. Hangar: situate.
I slid off its green surface like a mirror sheds spit.
How I loved that dreamed green on a blue sky and
popcorn clouded day, view from the bridge—it would
be mine! I snapped my fingers at things I did not like.

A life built on sand, not watching the tide come in,
heel-pounding dreamer awash, beached, forgetting, those
roots in *Breuckelen*, Broken Land, of millinery and starting over,
fur stitched in summer's sweat. *Geh weiter weg!*
How much more away could I get? Start over.

The spoked wheel flings landings about its rim then
gasp! air! first breath after thick sleep, dream draining
so quickly there's just a litter of empty envelopes and
accidents. Triangulate from one crash to the next, map it,
      part story,
            part weather and rock.

Name it home.

Colin Schmidt

Mr. and Mrs. Armstrong

It's 1969, and the moon has been alone forever
until now. Two men are holding each other
on the stairs of a space ship. From one breath
to the next, they listen to each other disappear.
Neil into the small lungs of his daughter,
dead on another planet. He swears he can see
his wife wade into the Ohio with a candle from here.
There's a plume of dust whirling in the white light
above his boots, flickering there in the kitchen
window of heaven. Janet lifts her night gown up
past her knees. The river silt a tinge electric in her toes.
The last few leaves rock quietly between the branches
and the grass. Each day since, a hole in the snowflake.
Each moment, a botched baptism. She watches the river
haul the clutter of night sky back between her legs,
thinking of how it's still yesterday on the moon, where
a child splashes around in a pile of glittering dust on the lawn,
how whatever's gone is still out there, somewhere.

JD Scott

Variations on an Attachment to

Leviticus

Who was concerned with the thread count? Were we too sleepy to be put to death? Blood was the color listed on the packaging, but to the eye it was more of a burgundy, some type of wine adhered to skin like we the mummies built of wax. Too red and ancient to be punished.

Leviathan

The bathtub was full of vinegar, but also honey. There was a toy pill that when placed in water, well, it grew into a gelatin shark. It was that toilet bowl sort of blue, and my entire tongue, how it slid up inside the gills. What we must have looked like from above.

Levigate

A room where no one eats. The green tile or the blue tile—which looks cleaner? When the sink leaked we skated on towels, spit into each other's mouths. There were fruit flies, or gnats, how you put a bowl of balsamic out to catch them. And too, motes, some allergen of longing.

Levisticum

People make too much meaning out of gardens. How I misheard lovage and thought this was confession. A basal rosette of leaves as shuriken. It was so tiny, the old bricks hovering over roots. And then I held you like a statue, and our clothes were locusts threaded together, alary to alary heart.

Levity   Hunger or love ache. There was a lightness to necking on the Edwardian. It was velvet and checkered, some hail-and-fire aesthetique. How sugardizzy I became from the Chambord. Who knew? It's not that I was agoraphobic. I thought there must be conquest inside these blueprints.

Levin   The porch swing gasping as frog. It's not that I was paid to remember a time before crone. Lightning. The lips moving in oyster. How we loved each other in every room of the house and knew this was enough. How if we stood still in the hallway, there was a trick mirror, our cardinal bodies in levitation.

Peter Sears

My Bigfoot Newsletter

My *Bigfoot Newsletter* comes every month. When it doesn't, I call in and often end up with two copies. I give one to Madge and Bill. They don't like the *Bigfoot Newsletter*, but they like to come over. I say, "How about a round of Rum Rockets?" "While you're at it, think about getting yourself a real job," suggests Bill. "And why haven't we seen that nice young woman again? We like her," proclaims Madge. Don't think

I haven't paused in the woods when I've picked up that rancid scent. For days I stutter, I want to veer off into the woods. I mention, "Carl Jung has much to say about Bigfoot." Madge responds, "Well, that is very nice of Mr. Jung, but I bet he has a good job and a nice family." "How about a Rum Rocket splash down on those ice cubes?" I say. Bill says, "Darn tootin." Madge adds, "Oh, who cares."

I like this story. I like the lead with the *Bigfoot Newsletter*. I used to subscribe. Madge and Bill I like for hounding me with dumb but important questions, like parents, and I like to invite them over because I am not going to drink alone, period. I want to let this story find its own way. I can see

how getting rid of Madge and Bill could become difficult. Madge smiles like a flowerbed, Bill chews on ice cubes. It gets me thinking of Bigfoot. I like Bigfoot, I like the idea of running hairy through the woods at night, scaring the hell out of people. Sure, a little juvenile, but easy

to get to when I'm carting round a ton of tenth-grade English papers to correct and coming home late and tired from coaching all afternoon, barely able to read anything but my *Bigfoot Newsletter*, while back and forth across my window sweep the pines towering over my house.

Jacquelyn Shah

—Qself, Jading

Soul, self; come, poor Jackself,
I do advise You, jaded, let be;
call off thought awhile...
    —Gerard Manley Hopkins

call it off   can you call it off   all dog thought
digging digging for bone wetting   your night brain
scratching your me-infested-me-infested hide
thought that pulls choke-collar-wise
till pop-eyed you're dog done   made dog   made dog again
and still boneless   still going on   look how you go on
cobbling some kind of something out of something
that grinds up your middle of the night
aren't you tired of it?
what is it   what is this Q of you you can't get over
get over it   this Q   this quixotic you that blacktops over the soft self
and skates   back and forth   back and forth   back and forth
rating the world   berating the world and its scoring scoring
corrugated overrated backsliding world   horror of porn and war
cankering worms   call it off   this whirring of your won't-let-go
this diggery doggery mad-dog frothing at the mouth   useless foam of a *no*
no-I-can't   when murdering is the loudest whirring
and night words cramp and crystal the mind
Q-infested-you-infested   bitten cur   kenneled in words
too damned faithful dog brain jading jading jading
whatever remains of your bitten-up soft-self . . .

Yudit Shahar
translated from the Hebrew by Aviya Kushner

Anew

I am creating myself anew
in simple words
asking for gifts
from the god of little mercies
asking not to surrender
to the evil words
that are born in darkness

I create myself
in the simple flavors:
hot bread and butter
coffee
morning light, scattering, spreading
through the window
as rain's paintbrush
washes the sky's blueness,

and in the nights,
between stomach and mattress
my body chokes on the echo
that insists on calling
your name
your name

Lee Sharkey

Spellbound
—after a painting by Samuel Bak

The capital burns on the horizon, tumbles into a chasm between land and land. So many dead, so many fled to this border shantytown, where we set up walls of wood scrap and cloth, scavenge food, shape beds of straw, prop up our gods. Soon it's a regular city. A chess set appears. A soccer ball. A dictionary. Twin decks of cards. For a moment a soft blue light suffuses everything. Already it seems we have lived here forever. A woman pulls up her skirt, feels for the gold coins in her hem. Children are laughing. A man fingers the watch in his pocket.

Alix Anne Shaw

Never Again an August Paradise

Now winter descends like a Puritan
with his lean, dry lips, his worsted
overcoat. Beneath it, he's all gristle, lashed

to bone. *Discipline*. We'll learn
to love his frigid house. Our hands
will be dumb clamps, our feet

two shriveled, yellow pups.
Each morning, he'll admonish us
against the heathen sky. Every night he'll read to us

the punishments of cold. We'll memorize
The Book of Cold. He'll force us to confess:
desire for the ember, lust for the fire's tongue,

for the lap of summer, profligate and green.
We'll learn to fear the hearthside. He'll wring us
wholly out. He'll whip our backsides

with his raw, red switch. We'll think we hate him. Secretly,
we'll come to love his glare. Beneath his blinding sky
we will feel clean. One day, perhaps, we'll wake

to find him still in bed, having died his silent
and imprecatory death. We'll chop through sod
to bury him, fling up lumps of mud. We'll keep his gravesite

empty, sweep it bare. Then, if a single crocus
pierces the frozen loam
we'll loathe the thing.

We'll never be free of his ghost.

Alix Anne Shaw

Truth operations / The most real day
5.442-5.4541

—*from* Rough Ground: A Translation of Wittgenstein's *Tractatus* from Philosophy into Poetry

She thinks that given a train car, there must be, from the start,

its holes and rust and all the other cars with which it will be linked

and the names of all the people who will ride inside the car

and the faces of the ones who fall from it. This tabulation

will be mathematical, exact. Like the outline of a gesture

a headlight might project across the dirt. There will be a finite set of ways

of climbing to the car and a certain set of houses it will pass.

Then one might count the people who clamor in the station.

One might count their suitcases, the seats they occupy.

There cannot be a different train, a different person

falling from a car. As a climbing body cannot both climb and fall

beside itself. (She thinks, one cannot say, *a body falls*;

one must say, *she falls, she has a name.*) As anyone pushed from a train car

has a name. As one who slips unfastened through the air

must think, *I am alone*. She thinks, these facts

are simple. She had suspected it: the most real day is the day one wakes to rain.

Kevin Simmonds

Exit Wound

stupid with prayer
(not a numbness / not
unfeeling)
I worked
at redemption
(force fed like that)

wept openly
at the ways I'd never
bend
spurs in my side
like anyone else
(is this how we're made?)

the seasons of my herding
before the slaughter
the escalation of weight
my mouth chewing always
the long cadenza
of cud

it was in the right lobe of the orbitofrontal cortex
a benign tumor
that got a father thinking
of touching children start
stockpiling
kiddy porn

it takes just
a little something
growing where it shouldn't be
to make us
wrongheaded
(isn't that breathtaking?)

wait
with me
for my monster
I'll wait
with you
for yours

~

when I return to the faith of my youth
I do so begrudgingly
impoverished in its ghetto
all those years then
the years of reversal
still warding off the hex the hook
in my every lip

but that *one* story
when Moses wants to see God
not just hear his voice
God agrees to *pass by*
but Moses would have to stay hidden
in the cleft of a rock
coming out only to see a trail
not unlike a billion starlings at his back

Kevin Simmonds

I don't remember
if Moses was satisfied
if he had cracked lips or hair loss
night sweats or aching
a creeping archipelago of melanoma & dry
heaves

but I do remember the opened window of water
for Peter
dreamy-eyed Jesus & the lasso
in his voice

~

across this saline drip
this sweet
electrocuting
water

walk

Brian Simoneau

Three-Year-Old Makes the Visiting Poet's Portrait

From the back of the hall, his voice a call to song,
        to singing, bringing to music whatever past we have.
                She slips from my lap when his voice passes along

something for her alone to claim, and she starts
        reshaping him, lines unsteady but pressed deep,
                reality what she knows best: the purity

of crayon to paper, prime colors the measure
        she makes of everyone, simple shapes. She tears it
                from her pad and runs to him, offers it up

for his fridge. He lays it down beside his books—mismatched
        stick-figure arms reaching out, mouth opened wide
                and the blue of his shirt the brightest in the box.

Joannie Stangeland

Gazebo

A rod, a rood, a perch of stones.
We measure land by the acre,
this earth a green woman asleep
deeply on her rumpled bed.

You and I dig through our stories,
watch them grow or let them lie
like tough husks
dormant in the soil's folds
until the woman dreams
and old slights or celebrations erupt—
a cloud of gnats,
cacophony of red and yellow flowers.

I scrape at what's unwanted,
weeds I can't name, consider
our lives rooted elsewhere, a garden
potted for less tending.
Oh, how I am tired today—

more than when we walked the tulip fields
and I saw color
without the dirt ground into my hands,
pictured a swath planted for you,

a table in the small house
I'd build without walls, a gift,
as if we'd sit there together
and understand the rain.

Joyce Sutphen

Reading Anna Swir in October

My suffering / is useful to me.

Now I understand why my friends
kept mentioning her name, and yes

I would like something useful
to come out of this.

I open my hand and there's
a bruise; I don't know where it

came from. I open my heart
and there's a riddle; I don't know

the answer. I can't remember
how it felt to be young,

and then I do. After that I
can tell you anything.

Jason Tandon

April Foolishness

Back by the vending machines
you bled and you bled.
For three hours we waited
to confirm what you had felt

slip beneath the green fluorescence
of a public restroom.
"A clot," the nurse would call it.
"A clot," the doctor would repeat.

One week later, after a spell
of spring weather, it snowed again.
Enough to brush the car. The rest
I left for the eventual sun.

We had stowed our boots in the basement.
Washed our hats and jackets, mittens and bibs,
and packed them with cedar
in a clear plastic bin.

John Allen Taylor

Monster

The frog moon erupts from the Atlantic,
& the fish begin to sing.

I move my body through surf & imagine foam teeth
dissolve me—

this, my most precious spell. Death is a blue burglar,
but I am vigilant.

I address the monster inside me, which is animal
& male: Do you remember

guiding my small hand over the quail's nest?
The stick & the squelching.

You were there at the birth of my terror—
made me to follow

my hands warily: my body the first cast stone
you named manhood.

May the surf unthread you from me. May you feel
a grief that swells

like flood waters between us: so the kelp will drift
& the fish not pause

& you diminish into whichever abyss
you choose.

Casey Thayer

Chucky Be Drowning

Reconstruct the reef: the staghorn,
bottlebrush, cat's paw, cluster coral—
and the underwater glow the moon
coaxed from the latticework undergirding.
For a single honors college credit,
we flippered through it, one-off cameras
dangling from our wrists, our breath
constricted to the nickel-width lifelines
of our snorkels. In my wandering,
I didn't give a thought to how easy
some smart ass could plug the tube.
I ignored the ease at which my air
could be cut off but not
Chucky, who scooted off the transom
of the trawler and couldn't kick enough
to keep his head above the waves.
Chucky be drowning, we ribbed him
after they back-slapped the water
from his lungs, the coughing stopped.
It became our refrain: *Chucky be drowning*
when he blanked one minute
deep into his demonstration speech,
Chucky be drowning when his safety
school said no, when he surfaced lit
and barely present for the last exam.
An unplanned kid later, post-shift
and three beers gone on his balcony,
he offered meth and needed me
to take it, a communion, initiation
into his religion of letting go.
I made an excuse, and the gulf
widened, and he floated farther away,

bobbed under, past the reef,
the sibilant Atlantic flux, the foam.
Below it, silence unfolded, a shoal
of bluehead wrasse scouting the bubbles
that marked my breathing, and the ones
beading from Chucky's mouth
that showed our teacher where to dive.

Casey Thayer

Metamorphosis with Drainage Pipe and *Playboy*

Ankle-deep in off-blue algal blooms
   from the city's overflow,
      your feet two luminous fish

become flippers, your lips
   purple in the milky late-light.
      Already your body begins to morph

before your older brother
   coughs, Knock it off,
      to a horsefly circling his head.

Past the mesh at the drainage pipe's
   open mouth, you tail a chalk-white,
      acned back & a loose pair

of cargo shorts. Side pockets stuffed
   with snuff you'll throw up
      down the sloped cement walls.

One boy unfolds the first vagina
   you've seen—ripped from
      a magazine—& holds his phone

open for light so you can study
   her pose. You focus on the hand
      she grips the bedpost with. Not sex,

but some hint of loneliness.
   How she looks past the camera.
      Then a second wave of nausea hits

from the hip flask of liquor or the pucks
   of Skoal he stole from Dad's gun cabinet.
      He'll know it's gone, you say,

as if you're talking to anyone.
   Lost between the V of her legs,
      the others don't hear. They've put up

with you enough. The cell phone
   blinks off, clicked shut & open,
      back on. The O of each boy's mouth

& you outside the glow. The terminus
   of your tunnel a headlight
      that grows larger with every step.

Robert Thomas

Sonnet with Schlock and Yonder

Multnomah Falls at Columbia Gorge:
sun slants down from the southwest and a gust
flares so the falls blow down from the southeast—
that *moment* when they converge in the pool
below, and we're staring into the core
of Oregon. God comes like that. Seven
seconds in Coltrane's *Love* that justify
the ways of love to man. Hardly ever
does it last that long. All the rest is schlock
and irrelevant. It was only three
seconds that I watched you taste the red sauce
as it simmered and I could see your eyes
thinking hard about something and my love
went deeper than the baby blue yonder.

Z.G. Tomaszewski

Chronicle

Wind: voice unshaped.
Every window ready to be a self-portrait.

I draw back my hand from god's pocket
to find the entrance stone.

I share the author's vision:
a cat goes missing and the religious search begins.

How squandering light leaves us
like an old man without his cane.

A bald woman loses
her hat and a moth lands there.

It's an incomplete history.
A clock under water.

The character notices a pipe leaking
along a dark, narrow hallway,

his cane at the other end.
A cat chases the moth

like slow undivided time.
And the woman whose life I do not understand

falls asleep on a bed of hats
while the old man approaches her window.

Sarah Viren

A Dialogue With Translation

*Eso es porque se trata de
un cielo que no es tuyo*
— Mario Benedetti

What is to be done,
My lifeline, with a heaven
That is also a sky
When it just won't do
Anymore to say something
Like the heavens?

I would advise you,
Sweetbread, to breathe
And consider that we
Are all arbitrary
And lined up
Like ducks to be shot.

But what really is
To be shot when you're
A word or twenty,
Like you are, my teaspoon,
Flaccid and abandoned
Of the memory of sound?

There is no bravery
In feigning deafness before
Our rows so sweet-kept
When we all know, crabcake,
That I live inside you
Like a burrowing worm.

It's true I can feel your
Tethering softness even
While you're chained elsewhere,
Fishtail, and I am still here-there
Before a sky as wide as lettuce
And bluer than a holy dome.

I am some heaven, and I am
That domed sky, and I am
Not that different, skylark,
From an inverted belly or a
Misplaced saucer except when
It comes being understood.

So tell me your name, taproot,
If it isn't earth cap
Or shouldn't be firmament
But is instead something
Simple like upstairs we have neighbors
Who never make a sound?

We could do this forever,
This back and forth, fruitcup,
Before we're forthright
Or somehow more right,
But we both know you're earthbound,
And I'll never be pinned down.

David Welch

The Afterlife

Maybe a petal from a tulip
floating on a pond. A salamander.
Maybe a river. Maybe a drop of water

in the eaves. Maybe a change
into the thought of change, the idea
that we will know

you're still here, our voices
clear in the air and moving
between the trees as if a leaf

traveling down toward its end
in autumn, the ground bracing,
the sound of its stem snapping

still high in the trees.
Maybe hammers. Maybe
ice under the cliff's orange rock

reaching down toward the earth.
Maybe nothing. Maybe nowhere.
Maybe the rabbit leaning on its leg

in the trap. Maybe nothing shows that
maybe marks the spot. Maybe everyone,
anyone, everywhere.

Joshua Marie Wilkinson

That's Where Both of You Were When I Slept

I was reading Ishiguro in bed
as an invalid when I heard you
at the kitchen table, typing about

your dead friend Hannah
the Czech novelist.

She had wanted to go to Pyramid Lake
and you had wanted to go with her.

But the book had fallen across my chest
and when I woke it was hail on the window.

You were in bed beside me studying
pictures on your phone of the ocean.

Mary-Sherman Willis

The Plot

A pine tree hisses
     Just a sea—with a Stem—
to make this earthly fragment
     the story of our short abidance:

     a hedged aesthetic, a garden plot,
a thing inside a thing;
its conflict, climax, revelation.

     Called Daisy, she preferred
Hemerocalis fulva, red daylily, cow lily.
     I am a lunatic about lilies—

in sunny clamor
     —the far theatricals of day
birdsong raucous fragrances
     whispers of passersby

beyond the hemlocks
     —there is a path
     just wide enough for two who love

to an arbor of honeysuckle roses
     a bee with a sting.
               Things
in a line becoming blowsy.

She, self-sown and weedy
     within her boundaries,
an index of earthly paradise.

Tim Wood

Shiki

Through the window,
a chiaroscuro of cumulus
lit up from inside.

Ototoi no
Hechima no mizu mo
Torazariki

The day before yesterday of
Gourd of water also
Didn't take,

Obi says,
There is no "I" in the poem.
So I say,

The water of the gourd
There for two days—
Didn't drink it.

Obi says,
Torazariki means
"take it" not "drink it."

Shiki lies on a mat
dying from tuberculosis.
The room white, well-lit

and small. He stares
at the ceiling.
The door slides open.

Tim Wood

First, the luminous
opacity of rice paper,
then the pink

of camellias
and the pinked,
bruised petals of

the azalea, the rusty shag
of barberry
and some lemony pear shapes

on the quince.
Beyond that,
the reddish, orange

conflagration of a maple
where gourds hang,
cut open to collect water,

the medicinal water
Shiki drinks each day
to help him breathe.

Among them,
one like the rest,
oblong and flesh-colored.

Shiki should have taken it
two days ago.
It hangs there still,

full and fixed
against black sinuous branches.
Shiki sees it.

No breeze.
Just the feeling of
light in the air.

And the heft
of the gourd
afloat in a day

impossibly bright.
It is not
about his need

but the gourd
he sees.
Not the water

he imagines, but this
peculiar excavated fruit-husk
useless and self-contained.

Shiki didn't think
that a poem should be a vessel
for personal expression,

Obi tells me,
as he scratches out the scene
on a yellow legal pad,

the ink accumulating
like clouds or boughs.
OK, I say,

Water gourd
Left there
Two days.

Jan Worth-Nelson

House Hunting

If I lived there I would have to be a witch,
casting out the evil done. Someone should write her
a sonnet, at least, the woman who met me at the door:
black eye, demented eye, body beaten through
the dry wall here, and here, and here, she said.
Three weeks to foreclosure, the closets smelled like
piss. We had a big dog, she said, he lived down here –
desolate cage swung open, dank floor swelled up like
a rotted boat. In a back room an old piano, carved rosettes,
upright and out of tune, of course. That stays,
she volunteered. I couldn't help it. I wanted
that house. I wanted its busted glass, black plastic
duct-taped windows, crooked cupboards closed with
bungees, flowered wallpaper dangling down in strips.

She said this year there were orioles in the weeds
out back, ripe pears on the riotous trees.

Shana Youngdahl

Week 2

We rustle.

The day crests
with two bottles of wine empty
by your chair. I'm half-awake.

The air thinks we're
bluebells opening in the rain
but what does it know?

Voices dazzle dawn's soft aches.

I'm nipple aware:
my body holds sunlight.

Shana Youngdahl

Week 4

Take this snow in hand. Take the moon
of it. If I feel fresh blood, begin

the task of mourning.

Today Julie's mother died
recall: swimming, warm kitchen tiles.

A town knows
about mothers. Today
I bleed quiet.

Theodora Ziolkowski

Girlhood Decorum

We did not realize the stakes in
the game we called "Lifeguard,"

how a pool of floating girls
might alarm our mothers.

Examining the piñata's severed
head, they wonder: What is this,

The Godfather? Happy birthday,
Miranda. You were so spent

trying to save us. Afterward,
you locked us in your room

until we agreed to play Ouija.
But if we really wanted to contact

the dead, we would have held
our breath longer. We would

have hugged our mothers.
We would have buried

the head of that trinket-
stuffed horse we socked

Theodora Ziolkowski

to a pulp, and in lieu
of making wishes on candles,

laid our fingertips on the planchette
and asked how much longer.

CONTRIBUTORS' NOTES

SAMUEL ACE is the author of *Normal Sex*, *Home in three days. Don't wash.*, and *Stealth*, with poet Maureen Seaton. He has received the Astraea Lesbian Writers Fund Award, the Firecracker Alternative Book Award, and is a two-time finalist for a Lambda Literary Award. His work has recently appeared in *Atlas Review*, *Mandorla*, *Fence*, *Posit*, *Troubling the Line: Genderqueer Poetry and Poetics*, and many other publications. samuelace.com

IRENE ADLER is the co-owner of a toy manufacturing business in Palo Alto, California, where she has also taught English. This is her first poetry publication.

ANNA AKHMATOVA (1889-1961) was sensationally popular during the teens and '20s of the 20th century, as part of the Acmeist movement, but after the Bolshevik revolution, her life and career went from crisis to crisis, and she was effectively barred from publishing. After Stalin's death, she was gradually rehabilitated and her work was again widely published in the Soviet Union.

JESSICA GUZMAN ALDERMAN is a Cuban-American poet from southwest Florida. Her work has appeared or is forthcoming in *Copper Nickel*, *The Normal School*, *Meridian*, and *Sonora Review*, among other journals. She reads for *Memorious*.

CATHERINE ALLEN is an anthropologist residing in Greenbelt, Maryland. She is author of *Foxboy: Intimacy and Aesthetics in Andean Stories* (University of Texas Press, 2011), a work of creative non-fiction, and co-author of an ethnographic drama, *Condor Qatay: Anthropology in Performance* (with Nathan Garner, Waveland Press, 1997).

STEVEN ALVAREZ is the author of three collections of poetry, including *The Pocho Codex* (Editorial Paroxismo, 2011), *The Xicano Genome* (2013), and *The Codex Mojaodicus* (Fence, 2017), winner of the Fence Modern Poets Prize. He has also authored two chapbooks, *Six Poems from the Codex Mojaodicus* (2014, winner of the Seven Kitchens Press Rane Arroyo Poetry Prize) and *Un/documented, Kentucky* (2016, winner of the Rusty Toque Chapbook Prize). His work has appeared in the *Best Experimental Writing (BAX)*, *Berkeley Poetry Review*, *The Drunken Boat*, *Fence*, *Huizache*, and *Waxwing*.

JOHN AMEN is the author of five collections of poetry; most recently, *strange theater* (NYQ Books). His poetry, fiction, reviews, and essays have appeared in journals nationally and internationally, and his poetry has been translated into Spanish, French, Hungarian, Korean, and Hebrew. He founded and edits *The Pedestal Magazine*.

MAJEED AMJAD (1914-1974) was a Pakistani poet and journalist who wrote in Urdu. His works have been published posthumously and his ghazals have been put to music by Pakistani artists.

DOSTENA ANGUELOVA is a poet, anthropologist, and journalist. She is the author of two volumes of poetry and has been published and translated widely throughout Europe. She holds a PhD in International Relations and is the author of the influential political nonfiction text, *Experts of Transition*.

JOSÉ ANGEL ARAGUZ is a CantoMundo fellow and a PhD candidate in Creative Writing and Literature at the University of Cincinnati. Author of six chapbooks and the book *Everything We Think We Hear*, he runs the blog *The Friday Influence*. His second book, *Small Fires*, is forthcoming from FutureCycle Press.

SHAUNA BARBOSA's poems have appeared or are forthcoming in *The Awl, Colorado Review, Virginia Quarterly Review, RHINO, The Atlas Review, No Tokens Journal, PANK*, and others. She received her MFA from Bennington College. Her first book, *Cape Verdean Blues*, is forthcoming in 2018 from Pitt Poetry Series.

SARAH BATES is a Creative Writing MFA candidate at Northern Michigan University. Her work has appeared or is forthcoming in *American Literary Review, BOAAT, So to Speak, The Normal School, Hobart*, and *Hotel Amerika*, among others. She currently lives in the Upper Peninsula of Michigan with her golden doodle, River.

JAKE BAUER is an MFA candidate at The Ohio State University, where he also serves as a poetry editor for *The Journal*. His work has appeared recently or is forthcoming in *DIAGRAM, The Bennington Review*, and *The Dunes Review*.

JEANNE MARIE BEAUMONT is the author of four collections of poetry, most recently *Letters from Limbo* (2016) and *Burning of the Three Fires* (2010). She teaches poetry in the Stonecoast MFA Program of the University of Southern Maine and at the 92nd Street Y in Manhattan.

ABIGAIL BECKEL is a poet and the publisher of Rose Metal Press, an independent, nonprofit publishing house for books in hybrid genres that she co-founded in 2006. Her poems have been featured in *Delaware Poetry Review, Open Letters Monthly*, and *The Fourth River*, among other publications. She lives in Maryland.

DEBORAH BERNHARDT is the author of *Echolalia* (Four Way Books) and *Driftology* (New Michigan Press/DIAGRAM).

MARY BLOCK lives and writes in her hometown of Miami, Florida. Her poems have been featured or are forthcoming in *Nimrod International Journal* and *Sonora Review*, among others. She is a graduate of NYU's Creative Writing Program, a 2012 Ruth Lilly Poetry Fellowship finalist, and a Pushcart Prize nominee. maryblock.net.

SILVIA BONILLA is the author of *An Animal Startled by the Mechanisms of Life*, published by Deadly Chaps in 2014. Her poetry and prose have appeared in *Fiction Now, Leveler Poetry*, and *White Ash Magazine*, among others. She has received scholarships from Slice, Vermont Arts Studio, and Tupelo Press. She lives in New York.

JUDE BRANCHEAU teaches Western literature and English composition at Ming Chuan University in Taipei, Taiwan. He received his MA in English from Miami University and his poems have appeared in *Southern Poetry Review, Indiana Review, Cold Mountain Review, North American Review, The Florida Review, Potomac Review*, and elsewhere.

MARK BRAZAITIS is the author of seven books, including *The River of Lost Voices: Stories from Guatemala*, winner of the 1998 Iowa Short Fiction Award, *The Incurables: Stories*, winner of the 2012 Richard Sullivan Prize, and *The Other Language: Poems*, winner of the 2008 ABZ First Book Poetry Contest.

JAY BRECKER resides in Santa Monica. His poems were published by *The Squaw Valley Review 2014* and the website onehundredwalkers.com. His chapbook "[dialog box]" was published by thistle & weed press. *A Case of Mad Love* was a semi-finalist in Trio House Press's 2015 manuscript open reading.

GAYLORD BREWER is a professor at Middle Tennessee State University, where he founded, and for more than 20 years edited, the journal *Poems & Plays*. His most recent book is the cookbook-memoir *The Poet's Guide to Food, Drink, & Desire* (Stephen F. Austin, 2015). His tenth collection of poetry, *Bird, Beast, & Flower*, will be published by Negative Capability in 2017.

MATTHEW BURNS teaches in upstate New York. His poem "Rhubarb" won a James Hearst Poetry Prize from *North American Review*; other poems have received Pushcart and Best of the Net nominations and have recently appeared or are forthcoming in *Posit, ellipsis…, Raleigh Review, Camas, Spoon River, Quiddity, LimeHawk*, and others.

CR CALLAHAN lives and writes in Auburn, Washington. He is a graduate of the University of Florida's writing program where he studied under Harry Crews, Smith Kirkpatrick, and Padgett Powell – so many years ago.

LAUREN CAMP is the author of three books, most recently *One Hundred Hungers*, winner of the Dorset Prize. Her poems have appeared in *Poetry International, Beloit Poetry Journal*, and as a Poem-a-Day for Poets.org. She is a Black Earth Institute Fellow and a producer/host for Santa Fe Public Radio. laurencamp.com.

CHRIS CAMPANIONI's new book is *Death of Art* (C&R Press). He teaches at Baruch College and Pace University. His "Billboards" poem responding to Latino stereotypes and mutable—and often muted—identity in the fashion world was awarded the 2013 Academy of American Poets Prize. He edits *PANK* and *Tupelo Quarterly* and lives in Brooklyn.

KAYLEB RAE CANDRILLI is author of *What Runs Over*, winner of the 2016 Pamet River Prize and forthcoming with YesYes Books, also serving as the non-fiction editor of the *Black Warrior*, with published or forthcoming work appearing in *Rattle, Puerto del Sol, Booth, Vinyl, Muzzle, The New Orleans Review*, and others.

JOHN RANDOLPH CARTER, Poet and Artist. Finalist: National Poetry Series. Poetry in journals including *Cream City Review, LIT, North American Review, Sewanee Review, Verse, Verse Daily*, and *Western Humanities Review*. Recipient of N.E.A., New York State Council, and Fulbright grants. Art in thirty-two public collections including the Metropolitan Museum of Art. johnrandolphcarter.blogspot.com.

ANDRÉS CERPA was raised in Staten Island, New York. He has received support from the McDowell Colony and the Bread Loaf Writers' Conference. His poems can be found in *The Kenyon Review, The Cider Press Review, Hayden's Ferry Review, The Bellevue Literary Review, Devil's Lake, Perigee*, and *West Branch*.

LEILA CHATTI is a Tunisian-American poet and fellow at the Fine Arts Work Center in Provincetown. The recipient of prizes from *Ploughshares'* Emerging Writer's Contest, *Narrative Magazine*, and the Academy of American Poets, her poems appear in *Best New Poets, Ploughshares, Tin House, Narrative, The Missouri Review, TriQuarterly*, and elsewhere.

NINA LI COOMES is a mixed-race writer born in Nagoya, reared in Chicago, now living in Queens. Her other work can be found in *the alice blue review, Blue Stem, taplitmag*, and elsewhere.

TOMMY D'ADDARIO grew up in Shelby Township, Michigan, and graduated from Hope College in 2016. He currently works as a chef on a dude ranch in the beautiful Sunlight Basin, Wyoming.

KRISTINA MARIE DARLING is the author of over twenty books of poetry. Her awards include two Yaddo residencies, a Hawthornden Castle Fellowship, and a Visiting Artist Fellowship from the American Academy in Rome, as well as grants from the Whiting Foundation and Harvard University's Kittredge Fund.

PETER DAVIS' books of poetry are *Hitler's Mustache, Poetry! Poetry! Poetry!*, and *TINA*. More info at Artisnecessary.com.

ADAM DAY is author of *Model of a City in Civil War* (Sarabande, 2015), and is the recipient of a PSA Chapbook Fellowship, and a PEN Emerging Writers Award. He directs The Baltic Writing Residency in Sweden, Scotland, and Bernheim Forest.

NANDINI DHAR is the author of the chapbook *Lullabies Are Barbed Wire Nations* (Two of Cups Press, 2015). Her poems have recently appeared or are forthcoming in *Chattahoochee Review*, *Grist*, *Tusculum Review*, *West Branch*, *New South*, and elsewhere. She is the co-editor of the journal *Elsewhere*. Nandini hails from Kolkata, India, and divides her time between her hometown and Miami, Florida, where she works as an Assistant Professor of English at Florida International University.

EMARI DiGIORGIO's first book, *The Things a Body Might Become*, is forthcoming from ELJ Editions. She's received residencies from Vermont Studio Center, Sundress Academy of the Arts, and Rivendell Writers' Colony. She teaches at Stockton University, is a Dodge Poet, and hosts World Above, a reading series in Atlantic City.

COLIN DODDS' fiction, poetry and essays have appeared in roughly three hundred publications, receiving accolades from luminaries including Norman Mailer and David Berman. Dodds' shorter work has been nominated for the Pushcart Prize and the Best of the Net Anthology, and his longer works have been finalists for the Trio House Press Louise Bogan Award and the 42 Miles Press Poetry Award, semi-finalists for the Horatio Nelson Fiction Prize and the American Zoetrope Contest. Colin lives in Brooklyn with his wife and daughter. See more of his work at thecolindodds.com.

RONALD DZERIGIAN resides in a small farming community just outside Fresno, California, with his wife and two daughters. He received his MFA from California State University Fresno and has been a recipient of the Academy of American Poets' Ernesto Trejo Memorial Prize and the C.G. Hanzlicek Fellowship.

MEG EDEN's work has been published in various magazines, including *Rattle*, *Drunken Boat*, *Poet Lore*, and *Gargoyle*. She teaches at the University of Maryland. She has four poetry chapbooks, and her novel *Post-High School Reality Quest* is forthcoming June 2017 from California Coldblood, an imprint of Rare Bird Books. Check out her work at: megedenbooks.com.

FLORBELA ESPANCA (1894-1930) was a Portuguese poet noted for the revolutionary eroticism and feminism of her work, notorious for her proclamations of "free love" in her sonnets and for public exposure of a condition of declining mental health, which ended her turbulent life in suicide at the age of 36.

NAOKO FUJIMOTO was born and raised in Japan. Her first chapbook, *Home, No Home*, won the annual Oro Fino Chapbook Competition by Educe Press. Her second chapbook, *Silver Seasons of Heartache*, will be available soon by Glass Lyre Press.

MICHAEL JOSEPH GARZA is a poet and activist from Cicero, Illinois, currently residing in Chicago's Hermosa neighborhood while writing and co-editing for *The Coup*. You can find him in every café in Chicago reading Wiman and Ciardi while finishing a Communications degree through Grand Canyon University.

ELLEN GOLDSMITH is the author of *Where to Look*, *Such Distances*, and *No Pine Tree in This Forest Is Perfect*, which won the Hudson Valley Writers' Center 1997 chapbook contest. A resident of Cushing, Maine, she is a professor emeritus of The City University of New York.

OMER HADŽISELIMOVIĆ was born in Sarajevo, Bosnia and Herzegovina, in 1946. Formerly a professor at the University of Sarajevo, he later taught English in Chicago and translated poetry. He passed away in December, 2016.

LOLA HASKINS has published fourteen books of poetry, most recently *How Small, Confronting Morning* (Jacar, 2016). Her prose work includes a poetry advice book, an illustrated collection of fables about women, and a book about Florida cemeteries. Among her honors are the Iowa Poetry Prize and two Florida Book Awards.

SARA HENNING is the author of *A Sweeter Water* (2013), as well as two chapbooks. Her work has appeared or is forthcoming in such journals as *Quarterly West*, *The Cincinnati Review*, and *Meridian*. Winner of the 2015 *Crazyhorse* Lynda Hull Memorial Poetry Prize, she serves as associate editor of Sundress Publications.

ANDREA HOLLANDER's fourth poetry collection was a finalist for the Oregon Book Award. Other honors include the Nicholas Roerich Poetry Prize, two Pushcart Prizes, and two fellowships from the National Endowment for the Arts. Writer-in-Residence at Lyon College for 22 years, she now lives and teaches workshops in Portland, Oregon.

MICHAEL HOMOLKA's poems have appeared in publications such as *The New Yorker*, *Ploughshares*, *The Threepenny Review*, *Poetry Daily*, and previously in *RHINO*. He is the author of *Antiquity* (Sarabande Books, 2016).

KATHRYN HUNT lives on the coast of the Salish Sea. Her poems have appeared in *The Sun*, *Orion*, *Rattle*, *Radar*, *Narrative*, and *The Missouri Review*. She is the author of *Long Way Through Ruin*, and has worked as a short-order cook, bookseller, food bank coordinator, filmmaker, and freelance writer. kathrynhunt.net.

ROCHELLE HURT is the author of two poetry collections: *In Which I Play the Runaway* (2016), winner of the Barrow Street Book Prize, and *The Rusted City* (White Pine, 2014). She's received awards from *Crab Orchard Review*, *Arts & Letters*, *Hunger Mountain*, *Phoebe*, *Poetry International*, and the Dorothy Sargent Rosenberg Fund.

SAFIA JAMA was born in Queens, New York, to a Somali father and an Irish-American mother. Her poetry appears in *Toe Good Poetry*, *Muftah Magazine*, and *The Offing*. Safia is a Cave Canem graduate fellow and the nonfiction editor at *Apogee Journal*.

WILLIE JAMES is a middle school teacher and an editor at *Pacifica Literary Review*. His work has appeared in *Mantis* and the *Breadline Poetry Anthology*.

BRIONNE JANAE is a California native, teaching artist, and poet living in Boston. She is a recipient of the 2016 St. Botoloph Emerging Artist Award. Her poetry has been published in *jubilat*, *BOAAT*, *Plume*, *Bayou Magazine*, *The Nashville Review*, and *Waxwing*, among others. Brionne is a Cave Canem Fellow.

LESLEY JENIKE is the author of *Holy Island*, to be released by Gold Wake in 2017, and *Punctum* (Kent State University Press), also to be published in 2017. She teaches at the Columbus College of Art and Design in Columbus, Ohio, where she lives with her husband and two children.

JOE JIMÉNEZ is the author of *The Possibilities of Mud* (Korima 2014) and *Bloodline* (Arte Público 2016). Jiménez is the recipient of the 2016 Letras Latinas/Red Hen Press Poetry Prize. His writing has recently appeared in *Entropy*, *Gulf Stream*, *Queen Mob's Teahouse*, and on the PBS NewsHour and Lambda Literary sites. He lives in San Antonio, Texas, and is a member of the Macondo Writing Workshop. For more information, visit joejimenez.net.

ERIN JONES holds an MFA in Poetry from the University of Florida. Her poems have appeared or are forthcoming in *Pleiades*, *Fourteen Hills*, *Passages North*, *The Journal*, *Moon City Review*, and elsewhere.

JASON JOYCE is a writer, designer, and arranger in Los Angeles who has made it a life-long mission to *never grow boring*. Originally from Wyoming, Jason puts his MBA to work as the co-founder of the clothing company Weekend Society, plays keys in The Rubbish Zoo, and loves ghost stories around the campfire. Choose your own adventure to find out more about his pursuits and published works: @jasonrjoyce on Instagram or jasonrjoyce.com.

KENDRA LANGDON JUSKUS is a writer and editor whose poetry has appeared in *Literary Mama*, *Ruminate*, *Fifth Wednesday Journal*, and the collection *City Creatures: Animal Encounters in the Chicago Wilderness* (UChicago Press). She is an associate poetry editor at *BOAAT* and lives with her family in Durham, North Carolina.

LEAH CLAIRE KAMINSKI teaches writing at UC Irvine and is assistant editor at new journal, *The Rise Up Review*; you can find her work in *Tupelo Quarterly*, *The Bellingham Review*, and *Catch Up*, and upcoming in *Witness Magazine* and *Vinyl*. Follow her sporadic missives on twitter @leahkaminski.

HOLLY KARAPETKOVA's poetry, prose, and translations from the Bulgarian have appeared recently in *Alaska Quarterly Review*, *Prairie Schooner*, *Drunken Boat*, and many other places. Her second book, *Towline*, is the winner of the Vern Rutsala Poetry Prize and is forthcoming from Cloudbank Books.

KARA KREWER grew up on an orchard in rural Georgia. She is currently a Wallace Stegner Fellow in poetry at Stanford University and holds an MFA from Purdue University. Her poems have appeared in or are forthcoming from *The Georgia Review*, *Prairie Schooner*, *The Journal*, *Prodigal*, *Ninth Letter*, and elsewhere.

PETER KRUMBACH was born in what used to be Czechoslovakia. Shortly after graduating with a degree in visual arts, he left the country, and began a journey that eventually took him to New York. He worked in commercial art, and later as a translator and broadcaster. His poems have recently appeared or are forthcoming in such places as *Alaska Quarterly Review*, *Phoebe*, *Columbia Poetry Review*, *Fugue*, *Serving House Journal*, and *San Diego Poetry Annual*. He currently lives in La Jolla, California.

AVIYA KUSHNER grew up in a Hebrew-speaking home in New York. She is the author of *The Grammar of God: A Journey into the Words and Worlds of the Bible* (Spiegel & Grau/ Random House, 2015). She is *The Forward*'s language columnist and an associate professor at Columbia College Chicago.

ARDEN LEVINE's poems have appeared or are forthcoming in *American Life in Poetry* (a project of The Poetry Foundation), *AGNI*, *The Missouri Review*, *The Carolina Quarterly*, *Rattle*, *Sixth Finch*, and elsewhere. Arden reads for *Epiphany*, holds an MPA from New York University, consults to nonprofit organizations, and lives in Brooklyn.

JEFFREY LITTLE is the author of *The Hotel Sterno*, *The Book of Arcana*, and *Five and Dime*. He is a 2001 Delaware Division of the Arts Poetry Fellow, and has published work in *Columbia Poetry Review*, *Exquisite Corpse*, *Forklift*, *Kiosk*, *Mudlark*, *Shattered Wig*, and *Swerve*, among others.

GINNA LUCK's work can be read or is forthcoming in *Juked*, *Gravel*, *Pif Magazine*, *Radar Poetry*, *Menacing Hedge*, *Gone Lawn*, *Hermeneutic Chaos Journal*, and others. She has been nominated for a Pushcart Prize and has an MFA from Goddard College.She currently lives in Seattle with her husband and three boys.

CODY LUMPKIN is currently a Visiting Assistant Professor of English at Marshall University, where he teaches film courses on the Marvel Cinematic Universe, *Star Wars*, and James Bond. He has had work published recently in *Prairie Schooner* and *Weber: The Contemporary West*.

DM MACORMIC is a PhD candidate at Oklahoma State University. His poems appear in *Smartish Pace*, *Mid-American Review*, *CutBank*, *Redivider*, *The Journal*, and *The Literary Review*. He is a recipient of the 2011 AWP Intro Journals Award for Poetry.

DON MAGER's chapbooks include *Drive Time* and *Russian Riffs*. He is retired from his position as the Professor of English at Johnson C. Smith University. In addition to scholarly articles, he has published over 200 poems and translations from German, Czech, and Russian. He lives in Charlotte, North Carolina.

LAUREN MALLETT was born in Lancaster, Pennsylvania. Her poems appear in *Tupelo Quarterly*, *Smartish Pace*, *Barrow Street*, *Sou'wester*, *Sugar House Review*, and elsewhere. She received her MFA from Purdue University and is the recipient of scholarships from the Indiana University Writers' Conference and the Indiana Writers' Consortium.

CYNTHIA MANICK is the author of *Blue Hallelujahs* (Black Lawrence Press, 2016). Her work has been published by the Academy of American Poets' *Poem-A-Day Series*, *African American Review*, *Bone Bouquet*, *Callaloo*, *Kweli Journal*, *Muzzle Magazine*, *Tidal Basin*, *Wall Street Journal*, and elsewhere. She currently resides in Brooklyn.

GAIL MARTIN's book *Begin Empty-Handed* won the Perugia Press Poetry prize in 2013 and was awarded the Housatonic Prize for Poetry in 2014. Her first book, *The Hourglass Heart* (New Issues Press), was published in 2003. She works as a psychotherapist in private practice in Kalamazoo.

CARLO MATOS has published four books of poetry and one book of fiction. His poems, stories, and essays have appeared in such journals as *RHINO*, *Handsome*, and *PANK*, among many others. Carlo has also received grants from the Illinois Arts Council, the Fundação Luso-Americana, and the Sundress Academy for the Arts.

BROOKE McKINNEY is a writer living in Roanoke, Virginia, with her loyal friend Max, a bulldog she has lived and traveled with for over a decade and who has endowed her with a greater understanding of love and survival. Her work has appeared or is forthcoming in *Appalachee Review*, *The Southeast Review*, *Columbia Poetry Review*, and *Artemis*.

RACHEL MENNIES is the author of *The Glad Hand of God Points Backwards*, winner of the Walt McDonald First-Book Prize in Poetry and finalist for a National Jewish Book Award, and the chapbook *No Silence in the Fields*. She teaches writing at Carnegie Mellon University and is a member of *AGNI*'s editorial staff.

FAISAL MOHYUDDIN teaches English at Highland Park High School in Illinois, is a past fellow in the U.S. Department of State's Teachers for Global Classrooms Program, and holds an MFA from Columbia College Chicago. His work has appeared in *RHINO*, *Prairie Schooner*, *the minnesota review*, *Poet Lore*, *Crab Orchard Review*, and elsewhere.

CAROLYN MOORE's four chapbooks won their competitions; her book *What Euclid's Third Axiom Neglects To Mention about Circles* won the White Pine Press Poetry Prize. She taught at Humboldt State University (Arcata, California) but is now a freelance writer working from the last vestige of the family farm in Tigard, Oregon.

JENNIFER MOSS is the author of *A Goat from a Distance* (forthcoming, Dream Horse Press) and of the chapbook, *Beast, to Be Your Friend* (New Michigan Press, 2009). She has published poems in *Hotel Amerika*, *Pleiades*, *Conduit*, *Denver Quarterly*, *River Styx*, and others, and has received grants from the Washington State Artist Trust and the Seattle Arts Commission.

BENJAMIN NASH has had poems appear in *Southern Poetry Review*, *The Cape Rock*, *The Aurorean*, *The Chaffin Journal*, and other publications.

ERIK NORBIE is a writer living in Minneapolis. His work has appeared or soon will in *The Examined Life Journal*, *Emerge Literary Journal*, and in collaboration with visual art.

OLIVIA OLSON is a librarian working in metro Detroit. A full list of publications and a wordy blog can be found at oeolsonblog.wordpress.com.

PABLO OTAVALO is from Cuenca, Ecuador, but now lives and writes in Evanston. A recipient of the 2013 & 2014 Illinois Emerging Poet prize, his work has recently appeared in *RHINO, Jet Fuel Review, Structo Magazine, Ninth Letter, Helicon, Tupelo Press, Sourland Mountain Review,* and *Glass Poetry Journal.* He's an avid chess player. He can be found at pablootavalo.com.

ERIC PANKEY is the author of many collections of poems, most recently *Crow-Work* (2015 Milkweed Editions). He teaches in the BFA and MFA programs at George Mason University.

CASEY PATRICK earned an MFA from Eastern Washington University and currently lives in Minneapolis. She's been awarded residencies from Hub City Writers Project and Tofte Lake Center. Poems from her first manuscript-in-progress have appeared or are forthcoming in *Pleiades, The Journal, Juked, Passages North, The Adroit Journal,* and others.

MILORAD PEJIĆ was born in Tuzla, Bosnia and Herzegovina, in 1960. Since 1992 he has lived in Sweden. He has published four poetry books— two of them are also available in English and one in German. He has published poems in several international literary magazines and in several languages.

SETH PENNINGTON lives in Little Rock, Arkansas, where he is publisher/designer at Sibling Rivalry Press with his husband, Bryan Borland. He co-edited *Joy Exhaustible* and *Assaracus,* and has new poetry forthcoming in *Lunch* and *Reading Queer: Poetry in a Time of Chaos.*

LIZZY PETERSEN served as the Managing Editor at *River Styx* for two years and now works as their Grant and Outreach Manager. Previously, she worked as the Poetry Co-Editor of *Sycamore Review* at Purdue University, where she received her MFA in Poetry. Her work has appeared in *Coldfront, FifthWednesdayPlus,* the Harriet blog, the *St. Louis Post-Dispatch,* and *Zócalo Public Square.* She teaches at Fontbonne University in St. Louis.

ROBBIE POCK was born and raised in rural Arizona, but is now a happy transplant to the Pacific Northwest. She writes, teaches, and raises her family near Portland.

ALISON PRINE's debut collection of poems, *Steel,* was chosen by Jeffrey Harrison for the *Cider Press Review* Book Award and was released in January 2016. Her poems have appeared in *The Virginia Quarterly Review, Shenandoah, Harvard Review, Michigan Quarterly Review,* and *Prairie Schooner,* among others. She lives in Burlington, Vermont, where she works as a psychotherapist.

DOUG RAMSPECK is the author of five poetry collections. His most recent book, *Original Bodies* (2014), was selected for the Michael Waters Poetry Prize and is published by Southern Indiana Review Press. Individual poems have appeared in journals that include *The Kenyon Review, The Southern Review,* and *The Georgia Review.*

REBEKAH REMINGTON's poetry has appeared in *AGNI* online, *Blackbird*, *Hayden's Ferry Review*, *The Missouri Review*, *Ninth Letter*, *Rattle*, *Smartish Pace*, and elsewhere. Her chapbook *Asphalt* (CityLit 2013) was selected by Marie Howe for the Clarinda Harriss Poetry Award. She is the recipient of a Rubys Artist Project Grant from the Greater Baltimore Cultural Alliance, as well as three Maryland State Arts Council Individual Artist Awards in poetry.

KYLAN RICE has poetry published in *West Branch*, *The Seattle Review*, and elsewhere. He has an MFA in Poetry from Colorado State University.

JOSÉ ANTONIO RODRÍGUEZ's books include *The Shallow End of Sleep*, *Backlit Hour*, and the forthcoming memoir, *House Built on Ashes*. His work has previously appeared in *RHINO*, *Poetry*, and elsewhere. Learn more at jarodriguez.org.

KATHLEEN ROONEY is a founding editor of Rose Metal Press and a founding member of Poems While You Wait. She is co-editor *of René Magritte: Selected Writings* (University of Minnesota Press, 2016), and her second novel, *Lillian Boxfish Takes a Walk*, will be published by St. Martin's Press in 2017.

KRISTEN ROUISSE holds an MFA in poetry from the University of South Florida. Her work has been awarded *Prairie Schooner*'s Glenna Luschei Award and The *Greensboro Review*'s Robert Watson Literary Prize, and is featured.

LEIGH CAMACHO ROURKS is a Fellow at The University of Louisiana at Lafayette. Her work has been awarded the Glenna Luschei *Prairie Schooner* Award and the Robert Watson Literary Review Prize and is featured in a number of journals, including *The Kenyon Review Online*, *Prairie Schooner*, *PANK*, *TriQuarterly*, and *Greensboro Review*.

SHIZA SOPHIA SABIR has translated some Persian works of Rumi, Hafiz, and Amir Khusrau, as well as many modern Pakistani poets into English. Her interest in literature ranges from Eastern and Western classics in English, Arabic, and Persian to contemporary French and Urdu poetry. She explores the effects of foreign poetic forms, such as the sonnet in Urdu or the ghazal in English, and is especially drawn to mystic themes.

DIANE SCHENKER's poetry has been published in *The Gettysburg Review*, *Subtropics*, *Gargoyle*, *Writers' Bloc*, and *The Squaw Valley Review*, among others. She is the author of the chapbook, *Relation/Couch/Dreaming*. Diane has worked and taught in theater and opera, and held various day jobs. She currently lives in New York City.

COLIN SCHMIDT grew up in New Jersey and Delaware and attends the MFA program at Rutgers-Newark. His current work can be found at *The Paris-American*, *Birdfeast Magazine*, and *The Cider Press Review*.

JD SCOTT is the author of two chapbooks: *FUNERALS & THRONES* (Birds of Lace Press, 2013) and *Night Errands* (YellowJacket Press, 2012). Recent and forthcoming publications include *Best American Experimental Writing*, *Prairie Schooner*, *Salt Hill*, *The Pinch*, *The Baltimore Review*, *Hotel Amerika*, *Barely South Review*, *The Atlas Review*, *Apogee*, *Winter Tangerine*, and elsewhere. JD can be found at jdscott.com.

PETER SEARS' most recent book is *Small Talk: New & Selected Poems* from Lynx House Press, 2014. He has published poems in *Saturday Review*, *Poetry Northwest*, *Mother Jones*, and *The Atlantic*. He recently stepped down as Oregon's seventh poet laureate. He lives in Corvallis, Oregon.

JACQUELYN SHAH is drawn to the quirky, the zany. Founding member of Houston arts organization *Voices Breaking Boundaries*, she has taught creative writing in schools. She has MA, MFA., PhD in English/creative writing and has published in journals such as *Cranky*, *Margie*, *Tar River Poetry*, *The Texas Review*.

YUDIT SHAHAR grew up on the border of Sh'chunat HaTikvah, or "the neighborhood of hope," in Tel Aviv. She is the author of the poetry collections *This Is Me Speaking* (2009) and *Every Street Has Its Own Lunatic* (2013), and recently won the prestigious Prime Minister's Prize in Hebrew Literature.

LEE SHARKEY is the author of *Walking Backwards* (Tupelo, 2016), *Calendars of Fire* (Tupelo, 2013), *A Darker, Sweeter String* (Off the Grid, 2008), and eight earlier full-length poetry collections and chapbooks. From the *RHINO* poem: Samuel Bak, a child prodigy imprisoned at age 9 in 1941 in the Vilna ghetto, continues to paint prolifically.

ALIX ANNE SHAW is the author of three poetry collections: *Rough Ground* (forthcoming from Etruscan Press 2018), *Dido in Winter* (Persea 2014), and *Undertow* (Persea 2007). Her work has appeared in *Harvard Review*, *Denver Quarterly*, *The Los Angeles Review*, and *New American Writing*. Also a sculptor, she is online at anneshaw.org.

KEVIN SIMMONDS is a writer and musician originally from New Orleans. His recent books include *The Noh of Dorian Corey* ドリアン・コーリーの能 (Galvez & Allen) and *Bend to it* (Salmon Poetry). He splits his time between San Francisco and Tokyo.

BRIAN SIMONEAU is the author of *River Bound* (C&R Press, 2014). His poems have appeared in *Boston Review*, *The Collagist*, *Crab Orchard Review*, *The Georgia Review*, *Mid-American Review*, *Salamander*, *Vinyl Poetry*, and other journals. He lives in Connecticut with his family.

JOANNIE STANGELAND is the author of *In Both Hands* and *Into the Rumored Spring* from Ravenna Press, plus two chapbooks and a pamphlet. Her poems have also appeared or are forthcoming in *Prairie Schooner*, *Cimarron Review*, *DMQ Review*, and other journals.

JOYCE SUTPHEN grew up on a farm in Stearns County, Minnesota. Her first collection of poems, *Straight Out of View*, won the Barnard New Women Poets Prize, and her most recent collection is *Modern Love & Other Myths* (2015). She is the second Minnesota Poet Laureate, succeeding Robert Bly.

JASON TANDON is the author of three collections of poetry including, *Quality of Life* (Black Lawrence Press, 2013) and *Give over the Heckler and Everyone Gets Hurt* (Black Lawrence Press, 2009), winner of the St. Lawrence Book Award. His poems have appeared in many journals, including *Beloit Poetry Journal, Columbia Poetry Review, Esquire, Paterson Literary Review, Poetry East, Poetry International, Prairie Schooner,* and on NPR's *The Writer's Almanac*. He teaches in the College of Arts & Sciences Writing Program at Boston University.

JOHN ALLEN TAYLOR's poems are published in *Booth, Nashville Review, Faultline, WILDNESS, Muzzle,* and other places. He currently lives in Boston and serves as the poetry editor for *Redivider* and the senior poetry reader for *Ploughshares*. He grows vegetables and brews kombucha. Say hello @johna_taylor.

CASEY THAYER is the author of *Self Portrait with Spurs and Sulfur* (University of New Mexico Press, 2015). He has work published or forthcoming in *AGNI, American Poetry Review, Poetry,* and elsewhere. A former Stegner Fellow at Stanford University, he lives in Chicago.

ROBERT THOMAS' most recent book, *Bridge*, was published by BOA Editions and received the 2015 PEN Center USA Literary Award for Fiction. His first book, *Door to Door*, was selected by Yusef Komunyakaa for the Poets Out Loud Prize, and his second, *Dragging the Lake*, was published by Carnegie Mellon.

Z.G. TOMASZEWSKI, born in 1989, lives in Grand Rapids, where he works maintenance at an old Masonic Temple and is a founding member of Great Lakes Commonwealth of Letters and Lamp Light Music Festival, respectively. His debut book *All Things Dusk* was the winner of the International Poetry Prize of 2014, chosen by Li-Young Lee, and published by Hong Kong University Press, and his chapbook *Mineral Whisper* is forthcoming from Finishing Line Press.

SARAH VIREN is a writer and translator. Her writing has appeared in *AGNI, The Iowa Review, Guernica,* and other magazines; *Ploughshares* Solos published her translation of the Argentine novella *Córdoba Skies* in 2016. She is managing editor for Autumn Hill Books, a translation press. More about her at sarahviren.wordpress.com.

DAVID WELCH has poems published or forthcoming in *AGNI, Boston Review,* and *Pleiades*. He's the author of a chapbook, *It Is Such a Good Thing to Be In Love with You* (The Laurel Review/Midwest Chapbook Series), and lives in Chicago.

JOSHUA MARIE WILKINSON is the author of a book called *Meadow Slasher* (Black Ocean 2017) and some other books.

MARY-SHERMAN WILLIS' books of poems include *Caveboy* and *Graffiti Calculus*. Her poems, essays, and reviews have been published widely. She is a graduate of the Warren Wilson MFA Program for Writers, has taught at George Washington University, and lives in Rappahannock County, Virginia. Visit maryshermanwillis.com.

TIM WOOD is the author of two books of poems, *Otherwise Known as Home* (BlazeVOX, 2010) and *Notched Sunsets* (Atelos, 2016). He is an associate professor of English at SUNY Nassau Community College in Garden City, New York.

JAN WORTH-NELSON lives in Flint, Michigan, where she and everybody else are still drinking bottled water. She taught writing at the University of Michigan-Flint, and edits East Village Magazine, a Flint-based monthly publication. Recent work has appeared in *MacGuffin*, *Midwestern Gothic*, and *Happy Anyway: A Flint Anthology* from Belt Publishing.

SHANA YOUNGDAHL is the author of *History, Advice and Other Half-Truths* (Stephen F. Austin State University Press 2012) and three chapbooks, most recently *Winter/Windows* (Miel 2013). She teaches writing at the University of Maine, Farmington, where she co-directs the Longfellow Young Writers' Workshop and oversees *The Sandy River Review*.

THEODORA ZIOLKOWSKI's poetry and prose have appeared or are forthcoming in *Glimmer Train*, *Arts & Letters*, *Prairie Schooner*, and *Short FICTION* (England), among other journals, anthologies, and exhibits. Ziolkowski is the author of *Mother Tongues*, winner of *The Cupboard*'s 2015 contest, and *A Place Made Red* (Finishing Line Press).

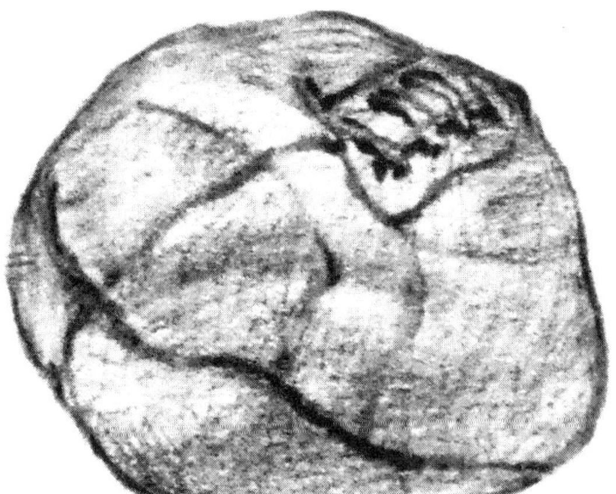

DONORS

Tony Adler
Michael Anderson
Barbara Barnard
Ellen Beals
Mary Biddinger
Bookends & Beginnings
Bryna Blustein
Prudence Brown
Debra Bruce
YZ Chin
Laura Cohen
Scott Cohen
Estate of Helen D. Cohen
Ann Cole
Ron Bedard and Bill Coughlin
Charles and Donna Dickinson
Jonathan Cohlmeyer and Margaret Edgar
John and Carol Eding

David Einhorn
Marc J. Frazier
Peter Fritzell
Reginald Gibbons
Gail Goepfert
Barbara Goldberg
Richard and Janet Goldberg
Joyce K. Gordon
Ralph Hamilton
Dave and Andrea Handley
Nancy Heggem
Stephanie Hochschild
Ann Hudson
Tim Hunt
Kate Hutchinson
David and Rochelle Jones
Ruth Kravitz
Michael Landau
Brenna Lemieux

Michael Lenehan
Jane Levine
David and Dianne Lipkin
Ronald Litke
Robert E. McCamant
Rose Parisi and Donald Meckley
Anne S. Merritt
Vernon A. Miller
Michael Miner
Roger Mitchell
Beverly Offen
Peter and Cheryl Olson
Liz Peterson
Roger Pfingston
Betsey and Dale Pinkert
Fran Podulka
Marcia Pradzinski
Jenene Ravesloot and Tom Roby IV
Christine Rice

Rob Rohm
Deborah N. Rosen
Carol Sadtler
Margaret Siber
Andrea Witzke Slot
Jessica Spring
George J. Stevenson
Liz Wescott and Chris Stoessel
Moira Sullivan
Neil Tesser
Naomi Thompson
Herbert K. Tjossem
Michael J. Tobin
Thomas and Jill Toffoli
Tony Trigilio
Kathy and David Umlauf
Kenneth L. and Sarah A. Vaux
Valerie Wallace
Marcia Zuckerman

The Antigonish Review
Annual Poetry/Fiction Contests

*Great Blue Heron
Poetry Contest
&
Sheldon Currie
Fiction Contest*

$2,400 in Prizes!

Fiction must be postmarked by May 31, 2017
Poetry must be postmarked by June 30, 2017

Entry Fee: $25.00 for either contest. This includes a one-year digital subscription to *TAR* which will begin with the fall issue, 2017. Make cheques or money orders payable to *The Antigonish Review*.

Mail submissions to: *The Antigonish Review* Contest, P.O. Box 5000, St. Francis Xavier University, Antigonish, Nova Scotia, Canada, B2G 2W5.

FOR FULL GUIDELINES: email TAR@stfx.ca, Phone 902-867-3962 or visit our website at <www.antigonishreview.com>.

Current issue of *Cloudbank*

Towline, by Holly Karapetkova, winner of the Vern Rutsala Book Prize.

CLOUDBANK

journal of contemporary writing

Submissions read year-round

Cloudbank 12 Contest
A $200 prize is awarded for one poem or short prose piece.

Vern Rutsala Book Prize
A $1000 prize, plus publication is awarded for a full-length manuscript.

Visit cloudbankbooks.com
for contest and submission guidelines.

Two-issue subscription—$15; Sample copy—$8

THE LOS ANGELES REVIEW

FICTION. POETRY. ESSAYS. REVIEWS.
SUBMIT. SUBSCRIBE.

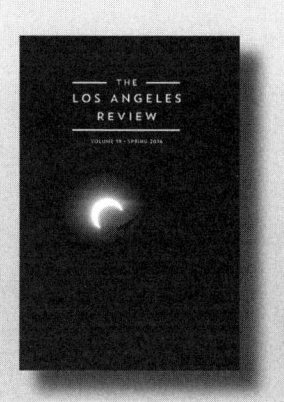

RED HEN PRESS

DIVERGENT, WEST COAST LITERATURE

VISIT WWW.LOSANGELESREVIEW.ORG
FOR SUBMISSION GUIDELINES.

Sugar House Review

AN INDEPENDENT POETRY MAGAZINE

Past Contributors:

Dan Beachy-Quick   Claudia Keelan   Paul Muldoon   Patricia Smith
Anne Caston   Cate Marvin   Carl Phillips   Janet Sylvester
Kate Greenstreet   Jeffrey McDaniel Donald Revell   Pimone Triplett
Major Jackson   Campbell McGrath Natasha Sajé   Joshua Marie Wilkinson

Work from our pages has been included in *Verse Daily, Poetry Daily,* and *Pushcart Prize: Best of the Small Presses,* 2015, 2014, 2013, and 2011.

SugarHouseReview.com